*Vagaries and Varieties
in Constitutional
Interpretation*

Vagaries and Varieties in Constitutional Interpretation

by Thomas Reed Powell

Legal Legends Series

qp

QUID PRO BOOKS

New Orleans, Louisiana

Vagaries and Varieties in Constitutional Interpretation

Published in 2012 by Quid Pro Books.

ISBN 978-1-61027-925-3 (pbk.)
ISBN 978-1-61027-924-6 (eBook)

QUID PRO BOOKS
Quid Pro, LLC
5860 Citrus Blvd., Suite D-101
New Orleans, Louisiana 70123
www.quidprobooks.com

Publisher's Cataloging-in-Publication

Powell, Thomas Reed, 1880-1955.
  Vagaries and varieties in constitutional interpretation / by Thomas Reed Powell.
      p. cm. — (Legal legends)
      Includes bibliographical note references, preface, foreword and index.
      Includes 2012 notes of the series editor.

1. Federal government—United States. 2. Judicial review—United States. 3. Constitutional law—United States. 4. Law—United States—Legal history. I. Title. II. James S. Carpentier Lectures. III. Series.

KF4550.A2 P65 2012   347.51'7—dc20
2012077653

CONTENTS

Page numbers in brackets below reference the original pagination (these numbers are embedded into text in this edition by the use of brackets). Page numbers shown to the right below (and without brackets) refer to the current pagination of this edition, found at bottoms of the pages.

Notes of the Series Editor
What to look for in this edition

As the series editor for *Legal Legends*, I have tried as much as possible to recreate the book as Thomas Reed Powell intended it in 1955: as an accessible collection published in 1956 from his James S. Carpentier Lectures presented at Columbia University in early 1955 (as posthumously finalized to print by Paul Freund and Ernest Brown). At the very least, formatting errors, poor scanning, notes, and missing words—all too common in such classic republications or digital reproductions—should not distract the reader from this great work, or make it hard to assign and reference.

We determined to make this edition as true to Powell's publication as possible. Yet the work must be usable today as well, to include digital publication and accounting for a contemporary presentation and current ebook technology. Producing this work for a modern audience and adding usable ebook formats required a few alterations that do not affect the substance but should be disclosed. Some notes to keep in mind:

- In this contemporary paperback, to facilitate research and citation uses of the work and possible classroom assignment, we have retained the original pagination of the 1956 printing (a numbering also consistent with later reprintings by other publishers). These numbers are here embedded into the text by the use of {brackets}, beginning with the body of the text at page 3.

- In ebooks, the footnotes are presented as endnotes, as in the digital universe they realistically must be. But they are linked in both directions to allow easy access for the reader. The footnotes are numbered sequentially throughout each lecture/chapter, just as in the original. In the new paperback edition, footnotes are presented as chapter endnotes and retain the original numbering, but are arranged in a more straightforward, vertical way than was seen in the original. They can be cited by referring to the pagination from the original printing, as embedded into our text, as of course the footnotes appeared on the text page inclusive of the reference number.

- We have made minor, consistent spacing changes throughout for legibility and without changing the words or quotability in any way (for example, deleting extra spaces around semi-colons or note references, and indenting block quotes to clearly set them off from normal text).

- The separate lectures are organized technically as chapters, as in the original. Readers should note, however, that the presentation was intended originally to be spoken, and it makes the most sense when read with that cadence and understanding in mind.

- The original Foreword by Paul A. Freund (the Harvard law professor who, with his colleague Ernest J. Brown, completed the book after the author's death), and Preface by William C. Warren (the long-time and influential Dean of Columbia Law School), are retained. Professor Freund's introduction is particularly incisive and witty, and worth a read. It was written soon after Powell's death and sets the table well for the book.

- We have omitted a long list of the previous Carpentier Lectures given at Columbia since 1904—including John Chipman Gray's 1907–1908 lecture series that became *The Nature and Sources of the Law*, which is also a new book in our *Legal Legends* Series.

- In a very few places where the original had an obvious misprinting, we took the liberty of correcting the printer error.

- This work is otherwise presented unabridged and without editing. The reference notes are presented, without editing, substantially as Freund and Brown completed them in late 1955. Although it is perhaps inevitable that some minor errors will creep into a re-publishing into new formats of a classic book, we have sought to minimize these as much as possible.

- The original Index is reproduced at the back. It refers to the original pagination of the book. We hope this feature proves useful to readers, and also allows ready reference to the original pagination for many concepts and entries.

This edition is available for multiple digital platforms using all leading ebook formats, where the gap in accuracy and availability is greatest. This modern and accessible paperback is also produced as part of the series, and parallels as much as possible the presentation found in our ebooks. All these formats are available at multiple bookseller sites online and at *www.quidprobooks.com*.

STEVEN ALAN CHILDRESS
Conrad Meyer III Professor of Law
Tulane University

New Orleans, Louisiana
September 2012

*Vagaries and Varieties
in Constitutional
Interpretation*

Foreword

IT WAS a happy inspiration that led Columbia University to invite Thomas Reed Powell to deliver the Carpentier lectures in April and May of 1955, as it is a sad turn of fate that requires this Foreword to be written by a hand other than his own.

Professor Powell was an indefatigable and articulate critic of the Supreme Court over a professional span of fifty years. So long as the Court was prepared to challenge, he was ready to respond, and this he did in a current of essays numbering close to two hundred. But he steadfastly forbore to compose a more systematic study; he was forever skeptical of generalizations and he had a low opinion of the merely expository—what he called deprecatingly *recitativo*. Moreover, in the spacious domain of constitutional law his interests were centered on certain specialized areas, notably the problems of national-state relationships in a working federalism, which lent themselves particularly to his kind of critical, pragmatic analysis.

In the present volume Professor Powell has not abandoned his preferences or relaxed his standards of self-criticism. The lectures are essentially a redaction or distillation of his most characteristic studies, many of which are to be found, or searched for, in highly specialized journals. But in the process of preparing six interrelated papers, the retrospective view has provided perspective as well and has enabled the author to reflect more generally and with a wider base than was possible in the course of earlier separate detailed studies.

It is altogether fitting that this undertaking should have been stimulated by the invitation from Columbia, for it was there, following his legal course at Harvard, that Professor Powell was exposed to the professors of political science, and they to him, in doctoral studies, and so became the *enfant terrible* of two disciplines. He remained to teach constitutional law at Columbia as Ruggles professor, serving for several years also as managing editor of the *Political Science Quarterly*, before going to the Harvard Law School in 1925. On the subject of his bi-professionalism he liked to quote the remark of his friend Robert H. Jackson, speaking at a meeting of the American Political Science Association in 1937, when Professor Powell was president of the Association: "Professor Powell stands high in the imagination of two professions. The lawyers imagine him to be a great political scientist, and the political scientists imagine him to be a great lawyer." It was at Columbia, too, that he came to know John Dewey; the congeniality of their thinking formed a close bond between them, as did also, it can be assumed of two Vermonters, pride in their common geographic background. Professor Powell never became a practicing philosopher; or rather, he became a more practicing pragmatist than the professors of pragmatism. Addressing a meeting of the American Philosophical Society he showed where he stood by confessing rather boastfully that he had read the first paragraph of every article published in the journal of that society in the preceding five years; his own address he entitled "How Philosophers May Be Useful to Society."

Like most good writing, the present volume can be read on two levels. It is, most directly, a study of the evolution and involution of constitutional doctrine. As such it will be of unique value to lawyers and judges who are required to grapple with problems of state taxation and regulation affecting the common national market. In paying his respects to the Restatements of the law, Professor Powell used to say that he could easily prepare a Restatement of Constitutional Law. In the usual form, the black-letter text would read: "Congress may regulate interstate commerce." A Comment would add: "The states may also regulate interstate commerce, but not too much." And then there would follow a Caveat: "How much is too much is beyond the scope of this Restatement." It is enough to say that "how much" is not beyond the scope of these lectures; it is their very substance.

On another level these lectures are an exercise in legal philosophy. I use the term exercise deliberately, for the lectures do not so much discuss a philosophy as they demonstrate it. The influence of Dewey, and through him of Charles Peirce, will be evident to those who bring a philosophical curiosity to the reading of legal literature. Definitions are to be formulated in terms of consequences; and when the consequences of a concept have been explored the need for a formal definition is likely to seem less insistent. Thinking about law is necessarily, to use a favorite word of Professor Powell's, judgmatical. A choice between the logical and the wise is generally a false antithesis, resting on an oversimplified premise drained of the relevant complexities of the problem. Logic of that sort he would picture in this way: "Other things being equal, as they never are, and in the absence of special circumstances, which alone create the problem, then. . ." The antinomies of constitutional law will yield to the principle of polarity, which finds elements of validity in opposed propositions and seeks to harmonize them through judgment in a particular context. The nation has powers adequate to its life; the states are sovereign in their sphere. Interstate commerce shall be free of state interference; interstate commerce must pay its way. These antinomies of federalism are at the heart of these lectures, and their scrutiny is given both closeness and depth, as I have suggested, by the double vision with which they are examined.

A few words should be added concerning the editorial function in preparing the manuscript for publication. After the lectures were delivered Professor Powell made some slight revisions in all of them. He marked the text with footnote signs but did not supply the footnotes themselves. When he was stricken in the late summer, as he was about to drive to his summer home in Westport, New York, his traveling bag contained the manuscript, which lamentably never received his final editing. In preparing it for the press, at the request of Dean Warren of the Columbia Law School, I have fortunately collaborated with my colleague Ernest J. Brown, who, like myself, was a student and later a colleague of Professor Powell and a successor of his in the course on Constitutional Law at Harvard, and who has a mastery of the varieties and vagaries that are the subject matter of the text. Our principal task has been to document the text by furnishing the footnote references, occasionally with some explanation. At a very few points in the manuscript we took occasion to correct a slip of memory or clarify an ambiguity that would not have survived the author's further scrutiny.

This is not the place for a personal appreciation of T.R.P. But it would be affectation not to indulge one's feelings at least to say that there is in these chapters an echo of that sharp gaiety and uninhibited candor that made companionship with T.R.P. a bright delight as well as a reminder that essential morality, the scrupulous morality of mind, need not be conveyed by solemnity. His wisdom, like that of Socrates himself, was sheathed in playfulness. That is certainly the most palatable kind of wisdom, probably the most telling, and perhaps the most profound. With Vermont sagacity Robert Frost has said "The way of understanding is partly mirth."

PAUL A. FREUND

Cambridge, Massachusetts
December, 1955

Preface

I T WAS INDEED wise and fortunate that the Faculty of Law of Columbia University invited Thomas Reed Powell to give the fourteenth series of Carpentier Lectures. Once he accepted the assignment to give the lectures in the fall of 1955, Professor Powell drove himself hard in preparing them, as though he himself realized that they were to be his last. We were all pleasantly surprised when he informed us that he could present them in the spring of 1955 if we desired. This we readily agreed to, and he delivered them with his charming and engaging wit. These last lectures represent the only unified treatment by Reed Powell as a teacher and a critic of the Supreme Court of the constitutional problems in a federal system—an analysis that he had developed over a lifetime dedicated to teaching.

It was appropriate that these last lectures were given at Columbia, where Professor Powell began his distinguished teaching career. The Faculties of Political Science and Law have traditionally been closely associated in the educational process at Columbia. Thus when Reed Powell accepted an appointment in the Department of Public Law under the Faculty of Political Science, he from the first assumed certain teaching duties in the School of Law. He became a member of this Faculty in 1913 and was later named Ruggles Professor of Constitutional Law. He found his association with members of the instructional staffs and students from the several faculties both stimulating and challenging, and he always liked to refer to Columbia as "an educational institution." Soon after the end of the lecture series, Columbia University conferred upon Thomas Reed Powell the honorary degree of Doctor of Laws during the 201st Commencement Exercises. I know that he considered that occasion to be one of the great moments of his life.

This book of lectures clearly reflects the important role that Professor Powell played in the development of constitutional law. He was both an effective teacher and a critic of the court. The task that he admirably fulfilled has been ably described by Mr. Justice Frankfurter:

> The task is admeasurement of judicial conclusions according to intrinsic coherence, to harmony with professed criteria, to consistency with invoked precedents and regard for relevant but unmentioned and unrejected precedents. These are at least

some of the factors by which judicial opinions call for testing. It can hardly be denied that T. R. Powell applied these valid tests to the decisions of the Supreme Court and their opinions more systematically, more searchingly, and more illuminatingly than any other critic of the Court's work during the last half century.

Professor Paul Freund who, in collaboration with his Harvard Law Faculty colleague Professor Ernest J. Brown, undertook to edit the manuscript of Reed Powell's lectures, has set the material in perspective in masterful fashion. I would like to take this opportunity to express to both of them our appreciation for the time, energy, and thought they gave in revising and filling out Reed Powell's lecture notes. Professor Powell told us that his notes were prepared for oral presentation and that some work would be necessary to put them in book form. Therefore I am sure that Professor Freund is very modest when he describes his work and that of his colleague as "furnishing the footnote references, occasionally with some explanation."

WILLIAM C. WARREN

April, 1956
Kent Hall, Columbia University

Vagaries and Varieties
in Constitutional
Interpretation

I. Establishment of Judicial Review

{*page* 3 *in original*}

THOSE OF YOU who recall how Topsy characterized her own genetic process may not be offended if I find a similarity between her origin and that of what we know as "judicial review." Such review of acts of a coordinate legislative body or executive authority was not conceived in terms in any of the early, post-1776 state constitutions, in the Articles of Confederation, or in the Constitution of the United States. Like Topsy, it just "growed."

For some time, however, the conception had been in the air before and after the Constitutional Convention of 1787. The possibility was not unknown to a considerable number of the members of that somewhat informally constituted political caucus or assembly, and research by Charles Beard has shown that a majority of the leading delegates favored the subjection of legislation to judicial inquiry and possibly control, and that they assumed that it was implicit in the institution they were proposing for adoption.[1] At any rate, whether favored or opposed, it was open as a possibility in the system. There was nothing in the proposal as approved by Congress and sent to the several states that in any way whatsoever, otherwise than by silence, negatived the power of the courts over legislation as it ultimately developed.

The absence of a grant of such a power to the judiciary might of course be deemed equivalent to a denial or prohibition {4} under the familiar conception that the new national government is a creature solely of the Constitution with no inheritance from predecessors. Unlike the states, which are deemed to be successors of British authority, the nation is *filius nullius* and has only such powers as find warrant in the words of the 1787 or 1789 charter. There is no "necessary and proper" clause broadening the powers of the judiciary as there is in the grant to Congress. So it could be only by inference or by conceptions outside the written word of the fundamental document that the power of judicial review could be assumed. I intentionally use the word "assumed" in two different senses: first, as inferred or implied, and second, as acquired by force or stealth and not as a duly vested donee.

Notwithstanding an awareness that judicial review was possible, among some of those interested there were two quite different views as to its nature. One view was a conception characteristic of the canon of sepa-

3

ration of powers. This was that the courts in the conduct of judicial business in settling disputes between litigants must decide for themselves independently whether the Constitution commands them or permits them or forbids them to disregard an act of Congress that seems to them to be in conflict with the Constitution. This was somewhat akin to their necessary burden of deciding between two possible interpretations of a single statute or between two statutes presenting possibilities of discrepancy or conflict.

Such a judicial resolution of difficulties presented by one or more statutes in no way precludes the legislature from enacting a different declaration for prospective application, or indeed for retroactive application, except for {5} two notions that this would invade the province of the judiciary or would infringe on some constitutionally protected private interests. These two notions are now ruling conceptions, but they were not initially necessary ones. And even now there are a few peculiar curative ways in which a legislature may alter the legal situation that would exist if subject solely to a prior judicial decree. This is exceptional, but I have in mind the *Wheeling Bridge* cases in which Congress by declaring a bridge a post road saved it from the condemnation that the Court had visited upon it as an unconstitutional state obstruction to interstate commerce.[2] Possibly the Wilson and Webb-Kenyon Acts present illustrations of somewhat similar restorations.[3]

The other conception of judicial review is that which is suggested by opponents who call it the "judicial veto." For this view there are judicial and scholarly declarations enough that the Court declares the statute to be void, and thus in effect expunges it from the books. An unconstitutional law is not law, and never was, say some judges and commentators.[4] But this, when true, is the product not of the judicial decree but of subsequent sufficient public acquiescence therein. It was not true in the succession of Supreme Court decisions on the power of Congress to compel the acceptance {6} of fiat paper greenbacks as legal tender. From a somewhat similar standpoint, it is not true when the condemnation is due to a judgment that in the special situation before the court the application of the statute would be unconstitutional.

An illustration of this appears in the judicial treatment of an ordinance of St. Louis apportioning the cost of a special assessment among the abutters in a somewhat complicated way. A moiety was assessed according to foot frontage, a method customarily approved. The balance was assessed according to area, with some variations depending on the depth of the lot and the distance to the street in the rear. The application to the lot of the first litigant was condemned by Mr. Justice Holmes as "a farrago of irrational irregularities throughout."[5] What could be worse than that? And yet, when another lot owner later objected to his assessment, he lost out because his lot was so shaped and bounded that the resulting charge of the farrago was less than what he would have had to pay under a straight foot-frontage rule.[6] The death of a statute under apparent judicial condemnation is dependent upon the reasons given, turning on whether they are confined to some particular application, and more broadly on whether subsequent decrees will remain in line or retreat or even retract or renounce.

Even among the protagonists and later supporters of judicial review there is certainly emphasis on the duty of others to accept the judicial condemnation. Hamilton in his famous 78th number of the Federalist Papers at one point says flatly: {7}

> There is no position which depends on clearer principles, than that every act of a delegated authority, contrary to the tenor of the commission under which it is exercised, is void. No legislative Act, therefore, contrary to the Constitution, can be valid.

And to the contention that "the legislative body are themselves the constitutional judges of their own powers, and that the construction they put upon them is conclusive upon the other departments," he answers that "this cannot be the natural presumption, where it is not to be collected from any particular provisions in the Constitution." There is something of question begging when Hamilton opines that it is the "will of the people" that the courts discover and apply, but he plants himself on what he regards as an undeniable premise when he says that "The interpretation of the laws is the proper and peculiar province of the courts."

Mr. Chief Justice Marshall in *Marbury v. Madison* reiterates that "It is, emphatically, the province and duty of the judicial department, to say what the law is."[7] He says also that "Certainly, all those who have framed written constitutions contemplate them as forming the fundamental and paramount law of the nation, and consequently, the theory of every such government must be, that an act of the legislature, repugnant to the constitution, is void."[8] When he adds that "the framers of the Constitution contemplated that instrument as a rule for the government of courts, *as well as of the legislatures*,"[9] he is open to the possible inference that each body is to interpret for itself, but this is by no means clear. The same inference might be drawn from his observation that judges and legislators are required {8} to take an oath to support the Constitution, but this again is not certain. Both to Hamilton and to Marshall, the dangers of legislative autonomy were repeatedly adduced in favor of judicial review as a power of complete condemnation.

It was some of the anti-Federalist adversaries, grudgingly conceding reviewing power in the courts, who confined it to drawing the demarcation of their own judicial orbit. The power of the judges to refrain from enforcing legislation which they deem unconstitutional does not in this view carry with it as a corollary any authority to dictate to others. This is well enough in a situation such as that in *Marbury v. Madison*, in which Marshall refused to accept a jurisdiction conferred by Congress but not in his judgment by the Constitution; but in other areas of judicial action the idea of the tripartite independence of each of the departments from its two companions would inevitably turn constitutional interpretation into a facsimile of a three-ringed circus. Doubtless even today there is occasional acquiescence in obedience to statutes that courts would declare unconstitutional, but when it takes a law suit to enforce obedience, denial of judicial enforcement is likely to impose a permanent frustration. Yet all that courts can do is to say something. The effect depends upon others. There are instances in which without a contest statutes have long been followed after similar ones of sister states have been condemned by the Supreme Court.

Two other impressions that I once entertained have been revised for me by my recent rereading of Beveridge and Charles Warren. I had assumed that Jefferson and Madison in fathering the Kentucky and Virginia Resolutions had {9} meant that the states through their legislatures were to have the exclusive power to deny application to acts of Congress. Their proposal was occasioned by their hostility to what the lower federal courts had done and said in enforcing the Sedition Act and in parading Federalist political speeches in charges to grand juries. But one or both of these two voluminous researchers have assured me that the progenitors of these Resolutions did not mean to deny to the courts the same power. I had long wondered, too, why these localists objected to the power of the courts to keep Congress within bounds, but now my recollection is refreshed that their resentment at *Marbury v. Madison* was aroused not so much by the judicial assumption of power to disregard acts of Congress as by the assertion of judicial power to coerce a high federal official in any proceeding in which the court has jurisdiction.

The party quarrels of the period have been detailed by Beveridge and Warren with such amplitude of quotation from Congressional debates, newspaper comments, and private correspondence, that all that should be repeated here is a stark outline of major doings, freed from the confusion of the plethora of print that these two tireless researchers give us.[10] The dying Federalist Congress passed the so-called Circuit Court Act less than a month before Jefferson's inauguration. This relieved Supreme Court Justices from further circuit court duty, and provided for six new circuit courts with sixteen additional judges, three circuit judges for five of the circuits and one for a western circuit. The {10} Supreme Court was to be reduced from six to five when the next vacancy should occur. It was disputed whether as many new circuit judges were needed, but on the whole the change was a wise one. President Adams hastily filled the new judge-ships with Federalists. John Marshall, still acting as Secretary of State, made out their commissions and they were duly delivered, though not with much time to spare.

In the new anti-Federalist Congress, a motion to repeal the Circuit Court Act was made on January 8, 1802. It passed the Senate by a vote of 16 to 15 on February 3. It passed the House by a vote of 59 to 32 and became law on March 31, 1802. This abolished the offices of the new circuit judges, restored the previously scheduled number of Supreme Court Justices, and reimposed on them the onerous peripatetic circuit duty, the restored circuit courts to be manned by one Supreme Court Justice and one District Judge. Three weeks later, Congress prescribed a significant change in the terms of the Supreme Court. Some of the dis-charged circuit judges sought to induce Congress to provide for a suit to raise the issue of their decapitation, but Congress did nothing, and no suit was brought. Marshall urged his Supreme Court associates to decline to do circuit court duty, but they thought, as was afterwards directly decid-ed,[11] that long acquiescence in the Judiciary Act of 1789 had sufficiently established the obligation so to serve. Marshall sat on circuit in Richmond and Raleigh during his Congressionally imposed respite from Supreme Court service.

To go back to the last days of the Federalist administration. On Feb-ruary 27, 1801, Congress passed the Organic Act of the District of Colum-bia, which provided for forty-two {11} justices of the peace. Adams made the appointments, and Marshall, still as Secretary of State, issued the commissions. They were, however, never delivered. Out of this failure arose the case of *Marbury v. Madison*. Four of these claimants to this insignificant office petitioned the Supreme Court for a writ of mandamus directed to Madison to compel him to deliver their commissions. At the December term of 1801 the writ to show cause was issued, returnable at the next term of court, which under existing law as laid down in the Cir-cuit Court Act of 1801 would begin in June, 1802. Meanwhile, however, on April 23, 1802, Congress provided that there should be no June, August, or December terms, but only February terms, so that the next term would not begin until February, 1803, fourteen months after the issue against Madison of the rule to show cause.

And so, on February 9, 1803, began the hearing in the famous case of *Marbury v. Madison*.[12] So far as I have ever found, no one had any prem-onition that the point of judicial review would be relevant to the disposi-tion of the controversy. From the rather full resume of the argument given in the case by the new Supreme Court Reporter, Judge Cranch, it seems clear that Mr. Charles Lee, former Attorney General and now counsel for the petitioners, was sincerely trying to get the Court to issue the writ. The new Attorney General, Levi Lincoln, who had acted as Secretary of State until Madison qualified, was called to testify, and he did his best to keep from the record a definite statement as to signing and sealing of the commissions and as to what had become of them. He was not sure of all the names on the commissions that he saw. He protested against high {12} officials being called away from their duties to testify. He said that he ought not to be compelled to disclose official secrets and that "he ought not to be compelled to answer anything which might tend to criminate him."[13] The Court assured him that he would be respected in these two particulars but insisted that he ought to answer.

The self-incrimination point has been thought to have been prompted by an apprehension that the witness might unwittingly commit some error in his testimony and thus be open to a charge of perjury. To one question, what had become of the commissions, the Reporter says that Lincoln objected to "answering fully." After he said that "he did not know that they ever came into the possession of Mr. Madison,"[14] the Court excused him from answering what became of them, because the point was not material if Mr. Madison never saw them. If Marshall were sincere in this, it would seem to afford a sufficient and compelling ground for ending the controversy. It would be improper to compel Madison to deliver what had never come into his possession. This invites a suspicion that Marshall had at this stage decided not to issue the writ. The proceedings, however, continued, and there was enough of testimony and affidavits from clerks in the Department to satisfy the Court that the commissions had been duly signed and sealed, which of course Marshall could have sworn to from personal knowledge, had he been a competent witness.

I should have admired Marshall more if he had in his opinion in *Marbury v. Madison* gone at once to the issue whether the Supreme Court had jurisdiction of the cause instead of indulging in his *obiter dicta* preliminaries. It has {13} long seemed to me unwarranted to declare first that these justices of the peace were duly chosen officers when their commissions had been signed, that they were therefore entitled to receive those commissions, that mandamus is a proper remedy to compel the ministerial act of delivery, and that a high executive officer like the Secretary of State is not immune from judicial coercion to perform ministerial duties, when all this was followed by the ruling that the Supreme Court is without jurisdiction in an original proceeding authorized by Congress when such authorization is not warranted by the Constitution. The Court of course would not be justified in exercising original jurisdiction in the case if convinced that Congress may not add to the original jurisdiction specified in the Constitution, and this conclusion would at once raise the issue of the judicial power to disregard legislation deemed unconstitutional.

Granting this preliminary position of inconsistency, Marshall had the choice of ruling either that he was bound by the legislation or was bound by the Constitution. The preliminary position, however, was by no means a solid one. Marshall might have held that Congress meant not to add to the Supreme Court's *nisi prius* original jurisdiction, but merely to permit the use of mandamus in exercising it. He might have held that there is no constitutional negative against legislative additions to the constitutional grant. His contrary view depended upon a negative pregnant, and such a pregnant is not always a fruitful conception. Thus neither the constitutional nor the statutory exegesis to find a conflict between the two was fully impeccable.

In affirming the power of the Supreme Court to declare the act of a coordinate body unconstitutional, Marshall {14} adds little if anything to the somewhat abler exposition of Hamilton in *The Federalist*. The premises are simple. The Constitution declares itself to be the supreme law of the land. It is not supreme unless it governs subordinate bodies not supreme. Though both of these statesmen seem to assume that a judicial finding of repugnance between the two laws is equivalent to an objective contradiction in the order of nature and not a mere difference of opinion between two different guessers, they both covered up this possibly question-begging difficulty by saying in somewhat different form that judges are expert specialists in knowing or finding the law. This assumes that all types of law are alike. The difference between judicial divisions in constitutional law cases and in private law cases may suggest that there is more than one kind of law.

It is true enough that common law and statutory interpretation present issues of public policy and of the analysis and appraisal of practical situations, as does constitutional law, but there still remain vital differences in the results of judicial determinations in these contrasting fields. Unwelcome common law and statutory interpretations admit of but slightly delayed prospective change by legislation. The correction of judicial infelicities in assuming constitutional negatives is much more difficult, whether by judicial recantation or by constitutional amendment. This may invite more extended comment later. It is also true that questions of fact and of public policy, though involved in various types of adjudication, vary greatly in the contrast between private law and public law. Determinations of purely common law issues do not involve the possibility of anything in the nature of a rebuke to other lawmakers than earlier or {15} alien wearers of the ermine. If there is, as some would have us believe, more of reason and less of will in judicial lawmaking than in legislation, the extent of the contrast may still be exaggerated.

On the issue of the wisdom of having judicial power as a possible brake on legislative power, I am ready to agree with Hamilton and only wish that I might put the point as effectively as he did. I cannot go along with him, however, in declaring that this does not imply superiority on the part of the judiciary but "only supposes that the power of the people is superior to both; and that where the will of the legislature, declared in its statutes, stands in opposition to that of the people, declared in the Constitution, the judges ought to be governed by the latter rather than the former." This mythical will of the people is to me as fanciful as the notions of emanations of concreteness from Olympus, Mount Sinai, or the Pythoness of Delphi. I prefer the frankness of Professor John W. Burgess who said in substance "I do not hesitate to declare that our form of government is the aristocracy of the robe, which I venture to regard as the best form of aristocracy in the world."

It seems somewhat strange that Hamilton thought that judicial interpretation reveals the will of the people, when he felt that the more direct expressions of that will come from those whom he called "the great beast." Marshall, at least in *Marbury v. Madison,* was not guilty of either of these ascriptions. He planted himself firmly on two postulates: (1) that the essential theory of a written constitution is that a law in opposition to the constitution is void, and (2) that "It is emphatically the province and duty of the judiciary to say what the law is." Only for confirmation {16} does he add that "the peculiar expressions of the Constitution of the United States furnish additional arguments in favor of its rejection," i.e., rejection of the doctrine that would ignore "the essential theory of written constitutions." And here he is far from fully happy. The fact that the Constitution requires the judges to take an oath to support it cannot go further than to warrant them to interpret it as a guide to their own action, because many other officers, state as well as national, are required to take a corresponding oath.

Neither Hamilton nor Marshall falls into the error of invoking the judicial power to condemn state conduct in conflict with the existence or with the exercise of national powers and contending that this implies a corresponding Supreme Court power over acts of Congress. The former judicial authority finds clear warrant in the so-called supremacy clause of the Constitution. The judicial power over national legislation cannot adduce support from the supremacy clause. Marshall seeks only some indirect support from it, though without overweening confidence. He puts it this way: "It is also not entirely unworthy of observation, that in declaring what shall be the supreme law of the land, the constitution itself is first mentioned; and not the laws of the United States generally, but those only which shall be made in pursuance of the constitution, have that rank."[15] The phrase "not entirely unworthy of observation" seems to say more to the ear than to the mind. Marshall had a flair for words as well as for thought.

Two further points about *Marbury v. Madison* invite notice. Was the declaration of the power of judicial review {17} important? Was it, even if unwarranted, an instance of judicial usurpation? To take the latter first. The question of this judicial power, even if it might have been avoided, was an open one under Marshall's chosen analysis. It was not *obiter dictum*, as was his consideration of the law of officers and of the nature of the writ of mandamus. If the question was an open one, which might have been answered either yes or no, is it usurpation to make a mistake, to give inadequate reasons or even to make a blundering judgment? It may be, as some one has said, that a blunder is worse than a sin, but neither may be usurpation. If one were to take the opposite view, one might find a wealth of judicial usurpation from judicial sins and blunders innumerable.

In the centuries of legal history, there arise many matters of first impression that may legitimately be dealt with in any one of two or more ways. If the conclusion proves acceptable to a sufficient number of qualified persons, it is likely to be repeated and possibly expanded. It may become a platform or a springboard or both. If, on the other hand, the outcome does not win sufficient acclaim, again among the qualified or perhaps even among the unqualified, it is, if I may jumble my figures of speech, likely to be devoid of procreative power, even if it still stands as a painted ship upon a painted ocean and solitary as upon a peak in Darien. It may be distinguished over and again, so as to invite the aphorism that a repeatedly distinguished case is a case that is no longer distinguished. This is what gives grist to law teachers. In the Supreme Court opinions, one may occasionally read of earlier cases that "it was there thought" or "it was there assumed" and then find some weak differentiation that is palpably a prelude to desuetude. I have sometimes {18} wondered why federal district and circuit courts do not in efflorescing *Erie R.R. v. Tompkins*[16] scrutinize a procession of state court opinions to find departures from or abandonments of earlier precedents sought to be concealed or evaded by flimsy differentiations.

Erosion of earlier legal doctrine may proceed to extinction. There may be legicide committed by a later court or by constitutional amendment. Such was the fate of an important decision rendered by the Supreme Court under Mr. Chief Justice Jay a decade and a week before *Marbury v. Madison*. This was *Chisholm v. Georgia*,[17] decided on February 18, 1793. With ample literary warrant in the language of Article III of the Constitution that the judicial power of the United States "shall extend to . . . Controversies . . . between a State and Citizens of another State" the Supreme Court by a divided vote held that this includes controversies in which a state is party defendant and a private citizen of another state is party plaintiff. An apprehension of this had been expressed by opponents of ratification of the Constitution. With the realization of such fears, opposition to the decision was rampant. The decision was never enforced, and shortly after it was delivered a constitutional amendment to recall it was proposed by Congress and duly ratified some five years later.

The characterization of the proposal as one to "recall" the detested decision is appropriate, for the Eleventh Amendment reads: "The Judicial power of the United States shall not be construed to extend to any suit in law or equity, commenced or prosecuted against one of the United States by Citizens of another State, or by Citizens or subjects {19} of any Foreign State." Thus the Amendment does not touch suits against a state by one of its own citizens when jurisdiction is premised upon the allegation that the suit is one arising "under the Constitution or laws of the United States." Nevertheless a unanimous court in *Hans v. Louisiana* in 1889[18] held that such a suit may not be maintained, though Mr. Justice Harlan confined his concurrence to the result, since he objected to Mr. Justice Bradley's criticism of *Chisholm v. Georgia*. This criticism may have been impolite to judicial predecessors, but the new case had to be based on a notion of state sovereignty that the *Chisholm* case had disregarded, notwithstanding its clear exposition in Mr. Justice Iredell's dissenting opinion therein.

Quite different was the later life of *Marbury v. Madison*. Though often criticized, the power there proclaimed has never been curbed by constitutional amendment. Various political proposals to curb it have been directed mainly, if not always, not against the existence of the power but against the manner or the finality of its exercise. There has been advocacy of the requirement of an extraordinary majority for judicial condemnation. There has been a proposal for the recall of an adverse decision by legislation. One was fathered by Senator Borah and one by former President Theodore Roosevelt. The senior Senator La Follette urged, as I dimly recall, a somewhat different device. President Franklin Delano Roosevelt sought amelioration in other ways and got it in another way than the way he planned. Wags have said that "a switch in time saves nine," and have quoted from Fielding: ". . . he . . . would have ravished her, if she had not, by a timely compliance, prevented {20} him."[19] There have been arguments aplenty that Marshall's assumption of the power was judicial usurpation, but they do not interest me. However initially indefensible that first seizure might have been, the power has now been duly sanctioned by a century and a half of sufficient national acquiescence.

The remaining question is: how important was it for Marshall to speak out as he did at the time when he did, and thus to assume a constitutionally conferred power of large magnitude when declining an insignificant legislatively conferred power? I do not fully share the views of Beveridge and Warren that it was of transcendent importance at the time it was rendered. The power was not again exercised until Taney's condemnation of the Missouri Compromise in holding that the due process clause of the

Fifth Amendment prevents Congress from forbidding slavery in the Territories.[20] This was a monstrous piece of judicial effrontery in the *Dred Scott* case, when the Northwest Ordinance had forbidden slavery and when free states, notwithstanding due process clauses in their state constitutions, had never had their power questioned. Taney may have thought that he could stifle sectional strife by his partisan promulgation, but he succeeded only in fostering what he meant to forestall. This, I venture to think, has not been the only instance in which this important Supreme Court power has been unwisely exercised. And there are differences of opinion as to how important it is. Mr. Justice Holmes, when on the Supreme Court bench, said in a speech at the Harvard Club of New York City: {21}

> I do not think the United States would come to an end if we lost our power to declare an act of Congress void. I do think the Union would be imperiled if we could not make that declaration as to the laws of the several states.[21]

With respect to the power over acts of Congress, Mr. Charles E. Hughes in the interim between his Associate Justiceship and his Chief Justiceship expressed the opposite view in his Columbia lectures on the Blumenthal Foundation. He said that "The dual system of government implies the maintenance of the constitutional restrictions of the powers of Congress as well as of those of the States. The existence of the function of the Supreme Court is a constant monition to Congress."[22] This was printed in 1928. Much has happened since. This is not the point at which to venture my comment, beyond saying that there is no doubt that Supreme Court power over national legislation served for a long season to imprison national power in conceptions that would have largely been congenial to the Framers of 1787 at that time for that time and perhaps for many periods later. Whether such imprisonment by judicial decree was a dictate of the Fathers or of the Congress of the Confederation or of an adequate moiety of the members of the state ratifying conventions is a matter upon which men and judges may differ.

My doubts as to the importance of Marshall's pronouncement are not related to what the Supreme Court has done from Mr. Chief Justice Marshall to Mr. Chief Justice Warren. They are based rather on the unprovable assumption that in due season the power would have been exercised {22} even had not Marshall made his affirmation in 1803. I cannot bring myself to believe that the utterance of one man concurred in by four colleagues can direct or control the course of history. The Supreme Court's power over state legislation was plainly if not explicitly indicated in the supremacy clause of the Constitution. State courts were exercising a similar power over state legislation under their state constitutions, and were certainly called upon to consider the legitimacy of acts of Congress before ruling that they had superseded the exercise of any conflicting power by the states. Such cases were bound to go higher. My confidence is the greater because I cannot be proved in error. Of course it may be questioned, because I cannot be proved to be right.

Should there be any lingering doubt about the constitutional warrant for the exercise of judicial review over acts of Congress, there can be no question as to the legislative warrant for it, if another provision of the Judiciary Act of 1789 was constitutional. For Section 25 of that Act clearly gave appellate jurisdiction to the Supreme Court in cases from state courts "where is drawn in question the validity of a treaty or statute of, or an authority exercised under the United States, and the decision is against their validity," or where state enactments are questioned as opposed to the Federal Constitution and laws and treaties, and the objection is denied. This provision, said the Supreme Court of Virginia, is unconstitutional. The federal courts may not dictate to state courts. The Supreme Court disagreed in *Martin v. Hunter's Lessee*[23] in 1816 in an opinion by Mr. Justice Story. For reasons of delicacy the Chief Justice did not sit. He had interests in other lands of the Fairfax devise involving some of the same questions. {23}

Here, by Section 25, Ellsworth and other members of the Judiciary Committee who had been members of the Constitutional Convention clearly affirmed the power of the Supreme Court to consider the constitutionality of national action when the issue was raised by state action. This means power to decide for or against the constitutionality of national action. The Supreme Court of Virginia denied the power of the Supreme Court to compel the state courts to carry out its mandate. Thereby they would declare the conduct of the Supreme Court opposed to the Constitution, if Congress indeed designed to authorize what the Supreme Court held that it authorized. Here was an opportunity for the Supreme Court to do something akin to what Marshall did in *Marbury v. Madison*, that is, to refuse to exercise the power claimed to be conferred by Congress and in the process to assert the power to declare the Congressional grant unconstitutional. Perhaps it was fortunate that *Marbury v. Madison* had avoided the necessity of any such later combination of humility and assertiveness in *Martin v. Hunter's Lessee*.

Notes

1 BEARD, THE SUPREME COURT AND THE CONSTITUTION (1912).

2 Pennsylvania v. Wheeling & Belmont Bridge Co., 18 How. 421 (1855).

3 These acts of Congress, making applicable to interstate shipments of intoxicating liquors the prohibition laws of the states of destination, though the Court had held such laws constitutionally inapplicable to such shipments, were sustained in *In re* Rahrer, 140 U.S. 545 (1891), and Clark Distilling Co. v. Western Maryland Ry., 242 U.S. 311 (1917).

4 See Norton v. Shelby County, 118 U.S. 425, 442 (1886), per Field, J.; COOLEY, CONSTITUTIONAL LIMITATIONS 259 (7th ed., 1903).

5 Gast Realty Co. v. Schneider Granite Co., 240 U.S. 55, 59 (1916).

6 Withnell v. Ruecking Const. Co., 249 U.S. 63 (1919).

7 1 Cranch 137, 177 (1803).

8 *Ibid.*

9 *Id.* at 179-80 (italics added).

10 The background of Marbury v. Madison is described in 3 BEVERIDGE, THE LIFE OF JOHN MARSHALL cc. 2-3 (1919), and in 1 WARREN, THE SUPREME COURT IN UNITED STATES HISTORY cc. 4-5 (rev. ed. 1926).

11 Stuart v. Laird, 1 Cranch 299 (1803).

12 1 Cranch 137 (1803).

13 *Id.* at 144.

14 *Id.* at 145.

15 *Id.* at 180.

16 304 U.S. 64 (1938).

17 2 Dall. 419 (1793).

18 134 U.S. 1.

19 Scholars will find the passage in Fielding's JONATHAN WILDE, Book III, chap. vii.

20 Dred Scott v. Sandford, 19 How. 393 (1857).

21 Holmes, *Law and the Court,* in COLLECTED LEGAL PAPERS 295-96 (1920).

22 HUGHES, THE SUPREME COURT OF THE UNITED STATES 95 (1928).

23 1 Wheat. 304 (1816).

II. Professions and Practices in Judicial Review

THE SO-CALLED distributing clause in Article 30 of Part One of the 1780 constitution of Massachusetts speaks in terms of prohibitions rather than in those of grants:

> In the government of this Commonwealth, the legislative department shall never exercise the executive and judicial powers, or either of them: the executive shall never exercise the legislative and judicial powers, or either of them: the judicial shall never exercise the legislative and executive powers, or either of them: to the end it may be a government of laws and not of men.

Or as John Dewey once put it in conversation: "to the end it may be a government of lawyers and not of men." This 1780 language is the classic statement of the doctrine of separation of powers, assumed to be the distinctive characteristic of American constitutions as contrasted with the fusion so common in other lands. The separation of course is far from complete, as it could not otherwise be. In the words of Judge Bynum of North Carolina in 1874:

> . . . while each [department] should firmly maintain the essential powers belonging to it, it cannot be forgotten that the three co-ordinate parts constitute one brotherhood, whose common trust requires a mutual toleration of the occupancy of what seems to be a "common because of vicinage," bordering the domains of each.[1]

{25} From the standpoint of the judiciary, there are two sides to the shield of the doctrine of separation of powers. It is essentially the province of judges to know what the law is, but judges should not undertake nonjudicial jobs. This latter injunction found expression a decade before *Marbury v. Madison*. Congress asked the circuit courts to pass on some pension claims and to report to the Secretary of War in an advisory capacity only, since the Secretary did not have to sanction the view of the judges. The Supreme Court in *Hayburn's* case[2] hesitated to accept this assignment and postponed action till the succeeding term. In the interim Congress substituted a different plan. In three circuits, the panels of two Supreme Court Justices and one district judge declined politely to act officially as courts, though in one circuit they offered to act as commissioners. Later the Supreme Court refused to issue a writ of mandamus against the Secretary of War to compel him to put on the list the names approved by the judges acting as commissioners. In still another case the Supreme Court indicated without giving reasons that the Justices were without authority to act as commissioners.[3]

These two sides of the shield may be so phrased as not to seem inconsistent. The judges will in proper cases act judicially, but they will not perform nonjudicial functions. From the standpoint of the practical administration of public affairs, the consistency may be thought to be an artificial verbalism. The Court may make pronouncements that the {26} legislature is not the authoritative judge of its own constitutional powers, but the legislature may not impose on the judiciary a task which the judiciary deems to be outside its constitutional powers. Thus in two ways the legislature is subject to judicial curbs. A naive observer might be inclined to assume that this makes for the superiority or the supremacy of the judiciary. Hamilton, however, did not regard himself as naive. He had sufficient acumen to discover or at least to argue that neither arm of the body politic is superior to either of the others. All difficulties vanish, all doubts are resolved, when we appreciate with Hamilton that the judicial hand on the helm of the ship of state means only that the power of the people is superior to the powers of both the legislature and the judiciary.

This view of Hamilton's differs somewhat from Professor Burgess's characterization of our system of government as the aristocracy of the robe. It differs also, of course, from the Stuart notion of the divine right of kings. Simply stated, it boils down to an assertion that "judges know best." It has to my mind never been put more felicitously than by Lord Coke in *Prohibitions del Roy*[4] in 1607. The Report concludes by saying:

> Then the King said, that he thought the law was founded upon reason, and that he and others had reason, as well as the Judges: to which it was answered by me, that true it was, that God had endowed his Majesty with excellent science, and great endowments of nature; but his Majesty was not learned in the laws of his realm of England, and causes which concern the life, or inheritance, or goods, or fortunes of his subjects, are not to be decided by natural reason but by the artificial reason and judgment of law, which law is an art which requires long study and experience, before that a man can attain to the cognizance of it; {27} and that the law was the golden met-wand and measure to try the causes of the subjects; and which protected his Majesty in safety and peace: with which the King was greatly offended, and said, that then he should be under the law, which was treason to affirm, as he said; to which I said, that Bracton saith, *quod Rex non debet esse sub homine, sed sab Deo et lege.*

For this Latin, my Lord Coke gives credit to Bracton. But Coke knew Latin himself, if I may trust a rumor re-ported to me by a scholarly Vermont judge some fifty years ago. He never gave me the source and I am quoting from memory. The tale was that Coke when hard pressed for a precedent to justify some novelty he was about to utter would write "As the old Latin maxim saith:" and then would invent the maxim. A judicial friend of mine once handed me the manuscript of a draft opinion, stating the facts and the conclusion and asking for suggestions of reasons and precedents. I feel confident that Coke knew that he was a participant in "the artificial reason and judgment of law" of which the king was innocent, for he invoked technical competence rather than the will of the people for the discovery of that "golden met-wand and measure to try the causes of the subject." Moreover, others, even before there was a constitution of the United States, have had insight. It was on March 31, 1717, that Bishop Hoadley said: "Whoever hath an absolute authority to interpret any written or spoken laws, it is he who is truly the lawgiver to all intents and purposes, and not the person who first wrote or spoke them."[5] This is a point that some clerics have been prone to gloss over by modestly attributing to another the views announced in their sermons. {28}

We may later invoke some twentieth-century official remarks from some Supreme Court Justices who seek to impress upon us in effect that it is not they that speak but the Constitution that speaketh in them. Somehow this reminds me of the biographer who wrote of Gladstone that his conscience was not his guide but only his accomplice. It will ever remain a mystery to me how intelligent jurists can make these professions of non-participation in the judicial process. Once I was misquoted in an undergraduate journal as having said that such men seemed to me either stupid or crooked. My colleague Edward Warren insisted that the false report should be corrected. So I wrote that the remark was made not about the Justices but about the things that they said, and I added that their professions must have been intended in some Pickwickian sense. I asked my colleague Warren what he thought of the judicial statements. He conceded that of course they were grievously in error. Later he voiced no objection when in a formal address I wrote that such judicial denials of personal power made me doubt either the capacity or the candor of the men who made them. I still doubt.

Before turning to similar Twentieth Century "judicialisms," something remains to be said about Marshall and his predecessors and contemporaries. In 1796 the Supreme Court decided the case of *Hylton v. United States*,[6] which had all the earmarks of a trumped-up dispute. An act of Congress imposed a tax called "An Act to lay duties upon carriages for the conveyance of persons." The issue in the case was whether this was a direct tax which has to be apportioned among the states according to population or an {29} indirect tax subject only to the requirement that it be levied on the basis of uniformity. The tax had been sustained as an indirect tax in the circuit court, and the Supreme Court unanimously affirmed in four separate opinions of those who sat: Chase, Paterson, Iredell, and Wilson. Ellsworth, the new Chief Justice, was sworn in only on the morning of the decision, and neither he nor Cushing had heard the argument, so neither participated. The technicalities may be left for a comment elsewhere, but here the remark of Chase is relevant:

> . . . it is unnecessary, *at this time*, for me to determine whether this court constitutionally possesses the power to declare an act of congress void, on the ground of its being made contrary to, and in violation of, the constitution; but if the court have such power, I am free to declare, that I will never exercise it, but in a very clear case.[7]

Two years later, in *Calder v. Bull*, Mr. Justice Chase repeated the statement that "I will not decide any law to be void, but in a very clear case."[8] He and his colleagues there held that the prohibition in the Federal Constitution against state *ex post facto* laws applies only to criminal laws and proceedings. So a statute of Connecticut ordering a probate court to grant a new trial was sustained. Chase, however, in the course of his disquisition declared that "An Act of the Legislature (for I cannot call it a law), contrary to the great first principles of the social compact, cannot be considered a rightful exercise of legislative authority." He enumerates hypothetical instances of such "clear cases," and says that "To maintain that our federal or state legislature possesses such powers, if they had not been expressly restrained, {30} would, in my opinion, be a political heresy altogether inadmissible in our free republican governments."[9] Here was an invocation of natural law without naming it. Mr. Justice Iredell disagreed:

> It is true, that some speculative jurists have held, that a legislative act against natural justice must, in itself, be void; but I cannot think that, under such a government any court of justice would possess a power to declare it so. . . . The ideas of natural justice are regulated by no fixed standard; the ablest and the purest men have differed upon the subject; and all that the court could properly say, in such an event, would be, that the legislature (possessed of an equal right of opinion) had passed an act which, in the opinion of the judges, was inconsistent with the abstract principles of natural justice.[10]

In my recent rereading of Marshall's major opinions, I find him substantially guiltless of absolving himself from the conclusions reached in the cases before him. In *Fletcher v. Peck*[11] in 1810, it is true, he adumbrated the possibility that there might be limits on legislative power *dehors* the written constitution, when he said: "It may well be doubted, whether the nature of society and of government does not prescribe some limits to the legislative power; and if any be prescribed, where are they to be found, if the property of an individual, fairly and honestly acquired, may be seized without compensation?"[12] But this is fairly oblique and may have been put forth as a sop to an amazing suggestion of Mr. Justice Johnson in his concurring opinion in the same case. This able Jeffersonian appointee to the high court proclaimed: "I do not hesitate to declare that a state does not possess the power of revoking its own grants. But I do it on {31} a general principle, on the reason and nature of things; a principle which will impose laws even on the Deity."[13] Unhappily there seem to be issues of jurisdiction and procedure here, which Mr. Justice Johnson leaves without explication. It must be doubted whether mandamus would lie. In my book the writ runneth not so high.

Marshall was such a born debater, such a skilled differentiator, and so ready to lay down lines of demarcation and to keep within boundaries beyond which, at least for the moment, he would not trespass, that he must have been fully aware that he was the monarch of what he surveyed and what he determined, and not the mere mouthpiece of some mysterious power. For all his firm convictions, he left fairly wide scope for play in the constitutional joints. States may not give an exclusive license for the use of steam on interstate waters, but they may stop insignificant navigation by authorizing a dam across a small tributary creek.[14] They may not tax the first sale in the original packages of imports from abroad, but they may tax the second sale or the first sale of a broken package.[15] They may not tax the currency operations of the United States bank, but they may tax such of their property as is not invested in United States bonds.[16] They may enforce state prospective bankruptcy laws where jurisdictional requirements are satisfied, but not retrospective ones.[17] I cannot believe that Marshall could {32} persuade others or even himself that he was not doing his own judicial work in his own way.

Behind this evidence from Marshall's judgments of constitutional play in the joints lie logical and philosophical insights into the process of judicial interpretation of a written instrument. In *Gibbons v. Ogden* he wrote:

> All experience shows, that the same measures, or measures scarcely distinguishable from each other, may flow from distinct powers; but this does not prove that the powers themselves are identical. Although the means used in their execution may sometimes approach each other so nearly as to be confounded, there are other situations in which they are sufficiently distinct, to establish their individuality.[18]

And in *Brown v. Maryland* there is a similar recognition of competing conceptions, positives and negatives, grants and limitations, motive power and brakes, which require keen judicial acumen to umpire between them in particular instances without commanding the same preference or adjustment in other situations. Here Marshall writes:

> The power, and the restriction on it, though quite distinguishable when they do not approach each other, may yet, like the intervening colors between white and black, approach so nearly as to perplex the understanding, as colors perplex the vision, in marking the distinction between them. Yet the distinction exists, and must be marked as the cases arise. Until they do arise, it might be premature to state any rule as being universal in its application.[19]

Here is wisdom which practical men apply in action, even when they may pontifically parade universals and absolutes in proclaiming justifications for what they do. {33}

To my shame, although these statements of Marshall were familiar to me from the days of my earliest teaching of constitutional law, I for some years failed to penetrate into their significance in judicial behavior. For a season I was perhaps less intent on judicial behavior than on fruitless efforts to catalogue and correlate those supposedly clear and settled principles in the verbal pronouncements of judges. Even when I had become aware that in the long run judges make law as well as find it, I had the notion that they laid their conceptual bricks from a perfect design to achieve the beauty of harmony and the *summum bonum* of the highest possible wisdom. And I suffered much in the process of trying to test particular decisions by their consonance with assumed, so-called general principles, and even more acutely by trying to test them by their consonance with each other. Was it my feebleness of mind, or were even judicial majorities somewhat errant or even perverse and foolish? The supposedly great teachers of common law subjects were able to paint pretty pictures and perfect geometric patterns. Why couldn't I do it in public law as they did it in private law?

My most poignant fumbling was in the topic of state taxation of interstate commerce. Why couldn't it be possible to reconcile the cases with that golden met-wand or measure of the law according to Lord Coke? Or was I perhaps trying to use natural reason instead of that artificial reason and judgment of the law? It was only after a season that my suffering was assuaged by what Mr. Justice Holmes said in *Galveston, etc. Ry. v. Texas*[20] in deciding whether a tax "equal to" a percentage of gross receipts from interstate transportation is as sinful as a tax "on" gross receipts from such {34} transportation. This is what he wrote:

It appears sufficiently, perhaps from what has been said, that we are to look for a practical rather than a logical or philosophical distinction. The state must be allowed to tax the property and to tax it at its actual value as a going concern. On the other hand the State cannot tax the interstate business. The two necessities hardly admit of an absolute logical reconciliation. Yet the distinction is not without sense. When a legislature is trying simply to value property, it is less likely to attempt or to effect injurious regulation than when it is aiming directly at the receipts from interstate commerce. A practical line can be drawn by taking the whole scheme of taxation into acount. This must be done by this court as best it can. Neither the state courts nor the legislatures, by giving the tax a particular name or by the use of some form of words, can take away our duty to consider its nature and effect. If it bears upon commerce among the States so directly as to amount to a regulation in a relatively immediate way, it will not be saved by name or form.[21]

This cannot be called a completely lucid formula which can automatically dictate answers. But it somewhat assuaged my self-distrust. I might try to resolve some of the confusion by the test of practical results rather than by tests of logic or philosophy. Even this test may not prove perfectly satisfying, as I may suggest later in dealing with the topic of state taxation of interstate commerce. Yet one may become satisfied not to be satisfied. It may be better for two cases to go in opposite directions than to have them both go in the same direction and so tip that side of the scales. The scales are more in balance if there are equal weights on both sides of the bar. Cases at polar points in opposite directions from {35} the equator are easy to differentiate and to explain. It is when the cases cluster close to the equator that the task of understanding and approval is harder. Yet somehow a line must be drawn. It should be a workable line in word and deed, in phrasing and in practicality, but care should be taken to keep the weights on either side of the line from becoming top-heavy.

If again I may be allowed to quote scripture to my purpose, again I resort to Mr. Justice Holmes, this time in *Hudson County Water Co. v. McCarter*.[22] Here he is talking about principles or canons of judgment, but he poses a problem akin to that of reaching particular results. Thus, as he tells us:

All rights tend to declare themselves absolute to their logical extreme. Yet all in fact are limited by the neighborhood of principles of policy which are other than those on which the particular right is founded, and which become strong enough to hold their own when a certain point is reached. The limits set to property by other public interests present themselves as a branch of what is called the police power of the State. The boundary at which the conflicting interests balance cannot be determined by any formula in advance, but

> points in the line, or helping to establish it, are fixed by decisions
> that this or that concrete case falls on the nearer or farther side.[23]

This is no more comforting to those who would sleep on a formula, free from thought, than was Holmes's earlier expression about seeking a practical rather than a logical or philosophical distinction. Such a point of view is anathema to a group of contemporary writers of a certain eschatological (the word must be spelled and pronounced correctly) persuasion who fill the law reviews with denunciation of {36} Holmes because he is skeptical about the dictates of "natural law," so called. Pious prattlers of an unanalyzed doctrine, they miss the greatness, the wisdom, and the ethical values of Holmes.

Once my good friend Mr. Justice Cardozo, who was an honor to Columbia College, to Columbia Law School, to the New York Court of Appeals, and to the Supreme Court of the United States, asked my permission to reprint in a volume of lectures a sentence of mine in a letter to him which said that "We should preach the gospel that there is no gospel that can save us from the pain of choosing at every step."[24] This of course is exaggerated. There are steps that a two-year-old can take without causing pain or thinking, but those are not the steps that greatly interest us in the law, private or public. If a precedent involving a black horse is applied to a case involving a white horse, we are not excited. If it were an elephant or an animal *ferae naturae* or a chose in action, then we would venture into thought. The difference might make a difference. We really are concerned about precedents chiefly when their facts differ somewhat from the facts in the case at bar. Then there is a gulf or hiatus that has to be bridged by a concern for principle and a concern for practical results and practical wisdom.

This is an attitude which forty years ago it was hard to get students to accept. It was not a dominant attitude in the Columbia Law School when I first taught classes there. It was certainly not good notebook stuff. Yet law students who wrote essays for the degree of Master of Arts found after a month of digging that they could not sleep on a formula. Perhaps the topics were diabolically chosen by the instructor {37} to emphasize the difficulty. In my youth I could be as mean as that. But the interesting thing was that after a few years in practice, these former grudging students found that the earlier unwelcome point of view explained the precedents and gave them a chance to escape from seemingly hostile generalities by pointing to distinctions and to practicalities and even to public policy, this public policy that was an intrusive anathema to my private law teachers in the Harvard Law School a half century ago. Yet how often it was that when these discerning practitioners made addresses as presidents of Bar Associations, they gravitated (the word does not imply rising) into the shibboleths of the eternal coercive, enveloping, and wholly beneficent law that *ex necessitate* shelters us all from chaos and destruction.

What is characteristic of constitutional law is familiar also in the field of private law, if we may again subpoena Oliver Wendell Holmes as witness. Over seventy years ago, in his lectures on *The Common Law* he told us:

> The life of the law has not been logic: it has been experience. The felt necessities of the time, the prevalent moral and political theories, intuitions of public policy, avowed or unconscious, even the prejudices which judges share with their fellow-men, have had a good deal more to do than the syllogism in determining the rules by which men should be governed.[25]

And later in the book he reiterates his position:

> On the other hand, in substance the growth of the law is legislative. And this in a deeper sense than that what the courts declare to have always been the law is in fact new. It is legislative in its grounds. The very considerations which judges most rarely mention, and always with an apology, are the secret root from {38} which the law draws all the juices of life. I mean, of course, considerations of what is expedient for the community concerned. Every important principle which is developed by litigation is in fact and at bottom the result of more or less definitely understood views of public policy; most generally, to be sure, under our practice and traditions, the unconscious result of instinctive preferences and inarticulate convictions, but none the less traceable to views of public policy in the last analysis.[26]

There are those who may say that this may well be true of the common law, in which there is no authoritative text to be interpreted, but that it does not follow that it is true of constitutional law or statutory interpretation. My thesis is to the contrary, though of course it concedes that there are appreciable differences of degree between the judicial freedoms in the two roles.

In the interest of fairness, those who disagree with the realism of Holmes should be given a hearing. In the famous or infamous *Lochner* case[27] which by a five-to-four vote held that labor in bakeries might not be limited by law to ten hours a day, Mr. Justice Peckham, after posing the due process dichotomy between the reasonable and the arbitrary, remarks that "This is not a question of substituting the judgment of the court for that of the legislature."[28] If the law is within the power of the state, it is valid, however much the judges might be opposed to its enactment. This is to say that if the law is constitutional, it is constitutional. If it is not, it is not. Thus is the circle completed. In this case the majority nestled a negative within the circle and allowed the opinion to say: {39}

> . . . we do not believe in the soundness of the views which uphold this law. . . . The act is not, within any fair meaning of the term, a health law. . . . Statutes of the nature of that under review, limiting the hours in which grown and intelligent men may labor to earn their living, are mere meddlesome interferences with the rights of the individual. . . .[29]

Had the limitation been to fourteen hours a day instead of to the unreasonable and arbitrary ten, it would, so far as appears, still have been a mere meddlesome interference with grown and intelligent men. This, however, would not substitute the judgment of the court for that of the legislature. Again we go to Holmes for wisdom; when in dissent he says:

> This case is decided upon an economic theory which a large part of the country does not entertain. If it were a question whether I agreed with that theory, I should desire to study it further and long before making up my mind. But I do not conceive that to be my duty, because I strongly believe that my agreement or disagreement has nothing to do with the right of a majority to embody their opinions in law.[30]

The *Lochner* case was later overruled by the *Bunting*[31] case without being mentioned at its own funeral. Yet in the *Adkins* case, which condemned an act of Congress indicating a floor below which factory wages for women workers might not go, Mr. Justice Sutherland said that the principles stated in the *Lochner* opinion "have never been disapproved."[32] This was true enough at the time, if all it meant is that liberty of contract may claim constitutional protection {40} and sometimes get it. If it meant more than that, it is open to serious question. Also open to question is Mr. Justice Sutherland's venture into judicial history when he says:

> This Court, by an unbroken line of decisions from Chief Justice Marshall to the present day, has steadily adhered to the rule that every possible presumption is in favor of the validity of an act of Congress until overcome beyond rational doubt. But if by clear and indubitable demonstration a statute be opposed to the Constitution we have no choice but to say so.[33]

His ensuing demonstration was clear enough, but far from indubitable. He dismisses declarations favorable to minimum wage legislation by saying that "they reflect no legitimate light upon the question of its validity, and that is what we are called upon to decide," adding that "The elucidation of that question cannot be aided by counting heads."[34] It is judicial heads that count. Five Supreme Court heads of the particular moment voted the condemnation, although thirty-five of the forty-five judges who sat in all courts on the question voted for validity. It was Selden in his *Table-Talk* who said: "They talk (but blasphemously enough) that the Holy Ghost is

President of their General Councils, when the Truth is, the Odd Man is still the Holy Ghost."[35]

It is again my favorite and much quoted judicial author who has said that on certain questions a page of history is worth a volume of logic.[36] These all too many pages of history on judicial notions of the nature of the judicial job are worth more than a library full of assertions that imply that {41} judges do not intrude personal views of policy in the process of interpreting the Constitution. Long ago that distinguished New York lawyer of a conservative cast of thought, Mr. James Byrne, pointed out that in a series of tax cases the Justices of the Supreme Court divided into exactly the same camps although the issues were so varied that one might have anticipated ample scattering. Some Justices were almost always for the taxpayer, others almost always for the Government. For years now, the newspapers have been giving the line-ups of Justices as they give the line-ups of legislators. Yet in spite of all this there is frequent reiteration of the myths that somehow the Justices are the mere mouthpieces of an oracle not themselves. The persistence of such fancies is not infrequently encouraged by utterances of the judges themselves. Yet the plain man can dispel the fancies with his simple knowledge of what actually happens.

The cotton- and grain-growing farmers knew what actually happened when by a six-to-three vote the Supreme Court declared the Agricultural Adjustment Act unconstitutional.[37] Railroad employees knew what actually happened when by a five-to-four vote the Supreme Court declared the Railway Pension Act unconstitutional.[38] They knew that if one or two Justices had voted the other way, the results would have been different, as they became different when changes in the statutes and changes on the Supreme Court bench sanctioned what had previously been condemned.[39] In the earlier cases Mr. Justice Roberts was anxious to assure both the farmers and the railroad workers {42} that it was the men of 1789 and not he who saved them from Congressional charity. "Our duty," he says, "is fairly to construe the powers of Congress, and to ascertain whether or not the enactment falls within them, uninfluenced by predilection for or against the policy disclosed in the legislation."[40] He finds the Railway Pension Act unconstitutional because it was for the benefit of the employees and not for the benefit of the railroads. It is a regulation of interstate commerce to help railroads but not to help railroad employees. This comes from the Constitution and not from any predilection of five Justices of the Supreme Court. If the railroad employees would only read the Constitution, they would see that this is so. They would be amazed that Mr. Chief Justice Hughes and Justices Brandeis, Stone, and Cardozo were not bright enough to know it.

The farmers also should have been glad to know that Mr. Justice Roberts was almost an automaton in finding that the Agricultural Adjustment

Act was opposed to the Constitution: "the judicial branch of the Government," he told them, "has only one duty,—to lay the article of the Constitution which is invoked beside the statute which is challenged and to decide whether the latter squares with the former."[41] The squaring process may involve the exercise of judgment, but it is doubtful whether this involves the exercise of anything that could be called power. "All the court does, or can do," explains Mr. Justice Roberts, "is to announce its considered judgment upon the question. The only power it has, if such it may be called, is the power of judgment. This court neither approves nor condemns any {43} legislative policy."[42] Of course all lawyers and students of constitutional law have known this for a long time. There was no need to call the point to the attention of any educated man. But Mr. Justice Roberts was evidently fearful that the farmers might not be fully aware of it. So he told them, and so they knew. They must have wondered how upon such a simple matter of judgment which could hardly rise to the dignity of a power, Justices Brandeis, Stone, and Cardozo should have failed to see that the statute and the Constitution did not square with each other. These dissenting three must have been without the right kind of precision instruments for measuring angles, areas and corners.

It sometimes seems that these judicial professions of automatism are most insistent when it is most obvious that they are being honored in the breach rather than in the observance. They seem to appear less often when statutes are sustained than when they are condemned, less often when the court is unanimous than when there is strong dissent. Try as I will, I cannot bring myself to admire both the candor and the capacity of the men who write such things to be forever embalmed in the official law reports. They must lack one or the other, or I must suffer from some such serious lack in me. There is a phrase of Professor Burgess's which has always puzzled me: he said of Calhoun and his adherents that "they were sincere or at least thought themselves so." If men sincerely think themselves sincere, are they not sincere, however much in error they may be? If the answer may be in the affirmative, then perhaps I should acquit these nonselfvaunting judges of lack of candor. But there remains another possibility. {44}

Of one thing happily we may be confident. There has never been any suspicion of lack of moral integrity in any Justice of the Supreme Court. Even in instances in which a judge here and there has been thought to entertain political hopes or ambitions, there have not, so far as I know, been notions that his votes on the Court have been influenced thereby. I am ready to assume also that no Justice has been without intellectual integrity even when he seems to me woefully mistaken both in his conclusions and in the reasons advanced in support of them. Doubtless there have been avoidances and evasions that would not be wise in a physical laboratory dealing with poisons or explosives, and some Justices have suggested privately that the necessity of securing at least four concurring colleagues has played a part in what the composer of the opinion has written or left unwritten. Some such inclusions and exclusions have been essential in many joint manifestoes. Judicial opinions not infrequently differ somewhat from scientific papers, but this does not necessarily convey an intimation of intellectual immorality even when they furnish welcome food for scholarly critics.

Of course judges may have passions and prejudices as do men of lesser breed without the law. Judges argue from undisclosed assumptions, as may you and I. Judges seek their premises from facts, also as you and I. They have preferences for social policies, even as you and I. They form their judgments after the varying fashions in which you and I form ours. They have hands, organs, dimensions, senses, affections, passions. They are warmed and cooled by the same summer and winter and by the same ideas as a layman is. This is one reason why it is well to have a bench {45} of nine Justices instead of only one. A composite judgment is likely to be safer and wiser than any possible product of an individual whim. One would hate to think of what might be said and done, if the issue were left exclusively to a counterpart of Mr. Justice McReynolds. And there have been other Justices who might be preferred as one of a group rather than as a sole dispenser of judicial divination.

In spite of Karl Marx, judges do not necessarily have class prejudices even when they hold to a creed that in varying seasons serves one group rather than another. Doubtless there may be habituations conferred by advocacy and counseling that may linger after donning the robe. Some Senators suggested that this might be true of Mr. Chief Justice Hughes and of Mr. Justice Stone, but their fears were at least greatly exaggerated. Mr. Justice Butler seemed to have retained some intellectual earmarks of his earlier railroad practice, though another railroad lawyer once observed that he would rather have Mr. Justice Brandeis's understanding of the railroad problem than Mr. Justice Butler's slant in his favor. Biographers of Mr. Chief Justice Fuller and of Mr. Justice Sutherland attribute their dominant attitudes to early environment and education, and some patterns of judicial behavior support their theses. But what of Justices Holmes, Brandeis, Stone, and Cardozo? The simplest explanation of their outlooks is that they had superlatively high-grade minds. This is always a help.

It would be interesting to speculate on the development of Mr. Chief Justice Stone from the time when he wrote his Columbia lectures on the Hewitt Foundation until the close of his career. As Dean of the Law School he was not {46} greatly amorous of new departures. Law was law, and the major and nearly exclusively task of a law school was the training of future practitioners and not the public display of the learning and talents of the faculty, as he once put it. What saved him from perhaps becoming a type of die-hard was his human feeling for his colleagues and his readiness to leave them free to do their work in the way they thought most important. He told me once that when I was suggested as a member of the Law Faculty, Mr. William D. Guthrie, who then lectured on constitutional law for an hour a week in one semester, asked him if I was "sound." Stone told me: "I assured him you were though I knew darned well you weren't, from his point of view." Stone's acceptance of views was in considerable part influenced by his respect or lack of it for the caliber and character of the men who advanced them. When one member of a sister faculty whom he did not respect denounced the *Ives*decision,[43] condemning the first New York Workmen's Compensation Act, he defended it on narrow technical grounds. When Frank Goodnow and Joseph Chamberlain, whom he greatly respected, spoke in criticism of the case, he was receptive to reconsideration. I recall other instances when suggestions which one year he did not favor would meet with partial or wider acceptance in the curriculum a year or more later. He always had a capacity for growth. There was never any question as to the strength of his brain power or the granite solidity of his character.

It was, I think, a good thing for his development that he was at the time of leaving Columbia fundamentally a common-law lawyer and not a public-law lawyer. He was {47} not filled with the conceptions that so long had dominated Mr. Justice Sutherland from the beginning of his public career. He was a master of the law of pleading and so of sticking to the issues properly presented. The declared issue in cases involving the problem of judicial review is that its exercise requires from the court a sincere respect for the legislative judgment. Such respect as a judge became characteristic of him, whatever he may have thought as a private person. Stone once told me that Mr. Justice Holmes had impressed upon him that it was not his function to try to play God.

In Stone's development after his appointment to the Court, a most influential factor was his admiration and affection for Holmes and his delight in their companionship. Their intellectual fellowship lay in the field of art as well as that of law. Nor would I discount the influence of Justices Van Devanter, McReynolds, Sutherland, and Butler, if I may speak as the billiard player who occasionally employs reverse English. It may seem strange to speak of the cooperation between these four colleagues and the succession of able graduates of the Columbia Law School who were devoted law clerks to the Justice who became Chief Justice. The students who wrote in law reviews were seldom like-minded with the Herbert Spencer who is reputed to have had such a dominating influence in the development of Mr. Justice Sutherland. The young men who went from Kent Hall to Stone's chambers in Washington year after year were an able law faculty, not only in technical law but in philosophical and social outlook.

I have not thought it necessary to dwell at any length on the vagaries and varieties of constitutional law as influenced {48} or determined by the particular composition of the Supreme Court bench at any given period. It is hardly necessary to dwell upon it. I can, however, hardly refrain from noting that it makes a difference. Had Stone, Brandeis, Cardozo, Holmes, Hughes, and the Ohio Mr. Justice Clarke been on the bench together, we could hardly have had the crisis of 1937. Well before that crisis, Roscoe Pound had pointed out how the philosophy of former centuries tends to become crystallized in judicial doctrine. This, he says, is the explanation of much in American judicial decision "which it has been the fashion to refer of late to class bias of judges or to purely economic influences";[44] and earlier he had written:

> Perhaps nothing has contributed so much to create and foster hostility to courts and law and constitutions as this conception of the courts as guardians of individual natural rights against the state and against society, of the law as a final and absolute body of doctrine declaring these individual natural rights, and of constitutions as declaratory of common law principles, anterior to the state and of superior validity to enactments by the authority of the state, having for their purpose to guarantee and maintain the natural rights of individuals against the government and all its agencies.[45]

Notes

1 Brown v. Turner, 70 N.C. 93 (1874).

2 2 Dall. 409 (1792).

3 The events are recounted in 1 WARREN, SUPREME COURT IN UNITED STATES HISTORY 70-81 (1926); United States v. Ferreira, 13 How. 40, 49-50 (1852); United States v. Yale Todd, decided in 1794, reported in Note, 13 How. 52 (1852).

4 12 CO. REP. *63, 65.

5 Quoted in GRAY, THE NATURE AND SOURCES OF THE LAW 125 (2d ed. 1921).

6 3 Dall. 171 (1796).

7 *Id.* at 175 (italics added).

8 3 Dall. 386, 395 (1798).

9 *Id.* at 388-89.

10 *Id.* at 398-99.

11 6 Cranch 87.

12 *Id.* at 135.

13 *Id.* at 143.

14 Gibbons v. Ogden, 9 Wheat. 1 (1824); Willson v. Black Bird Creek Marsh Co., 2 Pet. 245 (1829).

15 Brown v. Maryland, 12 Wheat. 419, 442-43 (1827).

16 McCulloch v. Maryland, 4 Wheat. 316, 436 (1819); Weston v. Charleston, 2 Pet. 449 (1829).

17 Ogden v. Saunders, 12 Wheat. 213 (1827); Sturges v. Crowninshield, 4 Wheat, 122 (1819).

18 9 Wheat, at 204.

19 12 Wheat, at 441.

20 210 U.S. 217 (1908).

21 *Id.* at 227.

22 209 U.S. 349 (1908).

23 *Id.* at 355.

24 CARDOZO, THE GROWTH OF THE LAW 64-65 (1927).

25 HOLMES, THE COMMON LAW 1 (1881).

26 *Id.* at 35-36.

27 Lochner v. New York, 198 N.Y. 45 (1905).

28 198 N.Y. at 56-57

29 *Id.* at 61.

30 108 N.Y. at 75.

31 Bunting v. Oregon, 243 U.S. 426 (1917).

32 Adkins v. Children's Hospital, 261 U.S. 525, 550 (1923).

33 261 U.S. at 544.

34 *Id.* at 560.

35 SELDEN, TABLE-TALK 141.

36 Mr. Justice Holmes, in New York Trust Co. v. Eisner, 256 U.S. 345, 349 (1921).

37 United States v. Butler, 297 U.S. 1 (1936).

38 Railroad Retirement Board v. Alton R.R., 295 U.S. 330 (1935).

39 Wickard v. Filburn, 317 U.S. 111 (1942); California v. Anglim, 129 F.2d 455 (9th Cir. 1942), *cert. denied,* 317 U.S. 669 (1942).

40 Railroad Retirement Board v. Alton R.R., 295 U.S. 330, 346 (1935).

41 United States v. Butler, 297 U.S. 1, 62 (1936).

42 *Id.* at 62-63.

43 Ives v. South Buffalo Ry., 201 N.Y. 271 (1911).

44 Pound, *The End of Law as Developed in Juristic Thought (II)*, 30 HARV. L. REV. 201, 210 (1917).

45 Pound, *The End of Law as Developed in Juristic Thought (I)*, 27 HARV. L. REV. 605, 626-27 (1914).

III. National Power

{49}

CONSIDERATION of the judicial development of the scope of national power must perforce begin with Marshall. Yet with the exception of decisions on the United States Bank and on the power of the Supreme Court to review decrees of state courts, Marshall's essays or sermons on national power were contained in opinions condemning particular exercises of state power. Marshall had been Chief Justice for over twenty years before he had a chance to make a pronouncement on the power of Congress over interstate commerce, although five years earlier he had sustained the power of Congress to charter the United States Bank. His latitudinarian view of the banking power in *McCulloch v. Maryland*[1] was an augury of what he was likely to do with respect to the national commerce power in *Gibbons v. Ogden*,[2] though the issues differed from each other.

The untutored view of the broad issue in *Gibbons v. Ogden* would be that it raised the question whether the mere possession of the commerce power by Congress precludes the states from exercising a similar power. The customary phrasing of this issue is whether the power of Congress is concurrent or exclusive. This, however, has nothing to do with the power of Congress in the sense of how far Congress may go. It has to do with the power of the states, that is, whether the states have a concurrent power with Congress or no power. This would have been an easy {50} question for the Framers to have settled by a negative on state regulation of interstate and foreign commerce. There is no such negative, although there is a qualified and partial negative on state taxing power affecting commerce and qualified negatives on state war-making and on keeping "Troops or Ships of War in Time of Peace." Moreover, the Constitution explicitly assumes the power of the states to pass inspection laws applicable to imports.

Marshall first poses the issue whether a New York statute granting an exclusive license to use steam on the waters of New York is "repugnant to the Constitution and laws of the United States."[3] The journey here involved was one between a point in New York and a point in New Jersey. This is ruled interstate from beginning to end. With a superabundance of argument, commerce is held to include navigation and not to be confined to trade. Commerce "among the several states" is "restricted to that commerce which concerns more states than one."[4] This is a much more expansive conception than "interstate commerce," which later was for a long time the ruling canon with the assumption that there has to be movement from one state to another to have "commerce among the several states." There was, however, movement here from one state to another, and one could hardly question that this steam-propelled journey is one within the commerce power of Congress if Congress chooses to deal with it.

Marshall in his opinion has not yet got to the issue in the case. He next tells us how far Congress may go. The "sovereignty of Congress," he says, "though limited to specified objects, is plenary as to those objects. . . ."[5] This power {51} "is vested in Congress as absolutely as it would be in a single government,"[6] with no subdivision into states. Marshall flirts with the idea that the commerce power of Congress is "exclusive," but he doesn't quite propose marriage. Like the umpire of a debate, he says that "There is great force in this argument, and the Court is not satisfied that it has been refuted."[7] It has since been refuted in part by explicit decision and clear declaration. No longer is it true in the sense adumbrated by Marshall, that when a state regulates the commerce subject to national power "it is exercising the very power that is granted to Congress."[8] This is contrasted by Marshall with the taxing powers of the state and the nation. They can both take bites from the same cherry. Without possibility of contradiction, Marshall says that "Congress is not empowered to tax for those purposes which are within the exclusive province of the states."[9] There may once have been taxing powers within the "exclusive" province of the states, but it would be hard to enumerate them now. Naturally, what is "exclusive" to either of the two governments is beyond the power of the other.

We have previously noted that Marshall lays down that two different powers may in many respects do the same thing or use the same means. He is compelled to recognize that the Constitution assumes the perpetuation of state power to inspect imports and exports. This power, however, is said to be not a commerce power but a power over police. If the word "semantics" were known in Marshall's time, it might properly be applied to his exercise in verbalisms. A little earlier in his opinion, in noting that the Constitution forbids the giving of preference to ports or requiring {52} vessels bound to or from one state "to enter, clear, or pay duties in another," he says that these are restrictions attached to a power over navigation, and invokes what is known as the *expressio unius, exclusio alterius* maxim by saying that "It is a rule of construction, acknowledged by all, that exceptions from a power mark its extent; for it would be absurd, as well as useless, to except from a granted power that which is not granted."[10] He does not, however, apply this canon of interpretation to the constitutional restriction on state power over imports. He escapes from it in two ways:

first, by noting that the restriction is on state taxing power and not on a power to regulate commerce, and second, though inspection laws have an effect on commerce, "that a power to regulate commerce is the source from which the right to pass them is derived, cannot be admitted."[11]

Contrariwise, the constitutional prohibition against giving any preference to ports says that "No preference shall be given by any Regulation of Commerce or Revenue,"[12] so that Marshall finds confirmation that the commerce power includes power over navigation. He does not note that there is another maxim for interpretation, namely, *ex majore cautela*—out of an abundance of caution. Restrictions do not indicate that outside the restriction there is power. They are put on to prevent erroneous assumptions that otherwise there is power. These are two wonderful canons of interpretation, each containing seeds for the desired result. Obviously, however, sometimes one is appropriate and at other times the other. If the choice should depend upon considerations beyond and outside the maxim, the maxim itself {53} merely points to a possible judgment and does not compel one.

After much of this discussion of concurrent and exclusive, Marshall makes it all irrelevant when he says that Congress has already regulated this commerce and rules that the state-granted monopoly is in opposition to the act of Congress conferring a coasting license on the offending vessel. In so deciding, he rejects the interpretation put upon the coasting license by Chancellor Kent and some other New York state judges. Marshall's exhaustive argument on this point leaves me unconvinced. The license to me is merely a certificate that the vessel as one of American registry is not forbidden to trade between ports of the several states. However this may be, the dispute shows how such able judges as Marshall and Kent may differ, and that statutes, as well as the Constitution, do not interpret themselves under their own steam. There could of course be no question that by reason of the supremacy clause in Article VI of the Constitution state statutes in conflict with valid Congressional acts lose the force of law so long as the national legislation remains on the books. There remains in other situations a different question, whether Congress has so occupied the field as to supersede even nonconflicting state statutes.

Marshall's next consideration of the commerce power is in *Brown v. Maryland*[13] three years later. Here he is much briefer, referring us to his more extended discussion in *McCulloch v. Maryland* on the power of Congress to charter a bank. *Brown v. Maryland* involved a state tax on the occupation of selling imported goods still in the original package. After condemning it as a forbidden duty or impost {54} on imports, Marshall also finds it in contravention of the act of Congress permitting importation. Taney as counsel for the state contended that the import loses its character on arrival and urged that a longer immunity would seriously hamper state fiscal power. To meet this, Marshall suggests various permissible state taxes such as those on sales of broken packages, on second sales, and taxes on sales at auction. The discussion of the commerce power of Congress is to the effect that it reaches beyond the introduction and extends to protect normal first sales. There was no act of Congress explicitly according such protection, but Marshall declared: "We think, then, that if the power to authorize a sale exists in Congress, the conclusion that the right to sell is connected with the law permitting importation, as an inseparable incident, is inevitable."[14]

This was questionable extrapolation from the Congressional customs regulations. One might perhaps infer that, after compliance with these, Congress would impose no further impediment to sale, but to find in silence a Congressional prohibition against state taxes on sale is somewhat imaginative. What interests us most at this point is whether Marshall would have held that Congress may go still further and prohibit such state taxes as he would allow to the states in the absence of any such prohibition, such as taxes on second sales and taxes on sales at auction. Presumably he would. Years later, in 1913, *McDermott v. Wisconsin*[15] held that Congress may require that labels prescribed by the Pure Food and Drug Act for goods shipped across state lines must remain thereon after the package has been broken and the containers remain unsold on the shelves of the retailer. {55} Without doubt, however, federal prescriptions are now with judicial consent applied both before shipment and after receipt to many intrinsically local matters that would have caused even the nationalistic Marshall to raise his eyebrows in his own day. To some of these we shall have occasion to refer. Yet from broad expressions in his leading opinions, support for such expansion may be derived.

In his *Brown v. Maryland* opinion, Marshall in effect incorporates by reference a considerable portion of his earlier opinion in *McCulloch v. Maryland*. Here was the strongest and ablest possible statement in favor of according a wide scope to powers granted to the nation. The nature of a constitution, he says, requires, "that only its great outlines should be marked, its important objects designated, and the minor ingredients which compose those objects be deduced from the nature of the objects themselves."[16] We should never forget, he adds, "that it is a *constitution* we are expounding."[17] A constitution cannot enumerate in detail all the means which may be used in exercising granted powers, for this "would partake of the prolixity of a legal code."[18] These are views put forth in favor of implied powers to choose the means of executing enumerated powers. It is not until later in the opinion that the great Chief Justice invokes the necessary and proper clause, insisting that it is an added grant and not a restriction on other grants. "Let the end be legitimate, let it be within the scope of the constitution, and all means which are appropriate, which are plainly adapted to that end, which are not prohibited, but consist with the letter and spirit of the constitution, are constitutional."[19] Thus "necessary and proper" becomes as life giving {56} as "convenient." When the Constitution adds restrictions to a grant, it knows how to do so, as when the power of the states to impose inspection fees is restricted to those which "may be absolutely necessary for executing its inspection laws."[20]

It might be precarious, as it hardly is important, to speculate whether Marshall a hundred years later would show equal cordiality toward the wide flood of national exercise of the commerce power and its companions which his successors have had to pass upon. Marshall's major decisions worked largely to the advantage of vested interests and the freedom of private business. His views were in accord with those of the Federalists and of their predecessors and progenitors who were leaders in the framing and the ratification of the Constitution. Would he feel as strongly nationalistic when national powers were wielded in favor of farmers, debtors, factory workers, the unemployed, the aging, the victims of accidents on land and on sea, the little children in the mills? Who knows? I do not. It is for me enough that Marshall's superb opinions afforded texts in support of many exercises of national authority for purposes undreamed of in his day.

Whether Marshall was in his own time eager for a wider exercise of national powers sanctioned by the tone of his essays is unknown to me. Something might depend upon the purposes of national proscriptions and permissions. At any rate, Marshall from the beginning of his Chief Justiceship was out of favor with the captains of the ship of state, and his persuasiveness would hardly have been potent. Whatever the reasons, there was little law on the national commerce {57} power until long after Marshall's day. In 1855 the Court sanctioned an act of Congress legalizing a bridge[21] that the Court had previously called an invalid state obstruction to navigation.[22] In 1865 the prohibition of a sale of liquor to an Indian in charge of a federal superintendent or agent was deemed a valid Congressional regulation of commerce with the Indian tribes.[23] In 1871 it was held that a federal license may be required of a vessel sailing on a navigable water of the United States and carrying goods entering and leaving the state, although the vessel itself could not cross the state boundary.[24] In 1876 the court sanctioned Congressional power to authorize a change in the channel of the Savannah River.[25] In the same year the Court assumed that Congress may provide for liability for violation of federal rules of navigation,[26] though Congress had not done so. In 1877 Congress was approved in regulating telegraph lines on military and post roads.[27]

Congress in 1789 passed a law providing that the regulation of pilots may continue to be in conformity with the laws of the states. In 1851 the

Court declared that Congress may not delegate *its* power to the states, and that therefore a subsequent state law has to have an independent basis of validity.[28] The first clear condemnation of a purported exercise of the national commerce power was in the {58} *Trade Mark Cases* in 1879.[29] Congress had not confined its regulation of trade-marks to those used in interstate trade. The Court held that the legislation had to be thus in terms so circumscribed, and it declined to decide whether even if so restricted it would be constitutional.

This may perhaps be the place to quote an observation of Mr. Justice Field in *Welton v. Missouri*[30] which condemned a tax which discriminated against the peddling of goods of past extrastate origin, even though the particular sales were not interstate. Speaking of the power of Congress, he said:

> It is sufficient to hold now that the commercial power continues un-
> til the commodity has ceased to be the subject of discriminating leg-
> islation by reason of its foreign character. That power protects it,
> even after it has entered the State, from any burdens imposed by
> reason of its foreign origin.[31]

Of course what the Constitution does of its own force, Congress may also do.

This is not an impressive array of decisions on the commerce power of Congress, as compared with the numerous restrictions imposed by the Supreme Court on the taxing and police powers of the states during the period prior to the nineties. It was not until the nineties that Congress began more far-reaching regulatory activities. Though the Supreme Court sustained both the Sherman Law[32] and the Interstate Commerce Act,[33] it was inclined to pare them down to the minimum that their language would warrant. The most unwarranted judicial offense was the ruling that {59} a substantial monopoly of ownership of stock in sugar refineries which sell largely in interstate commerce concerns merely manufacturing which is not commerce.[34] It took ten years for the Court to change its mind,[35] and meanwhile the so-called trusts grew and flourished. The framing of statutes with standards in constitutional phrases offers the court a leeway in statutory interpretation that may often exceed the freedom to condemn on constitutional grounds.

It has long been constitutional dogma that manufacturing, like agriculture, mining, education, and athletic exhibitions, is not intrinsically commerce. This has left them subject to state powers, both of taxation and police. It does not follow, however, that when these activities are to some extent dependent upon transportation Congress may not find a handle to restrict or to deny them the facilities of transportation to extrastate markets, as we now well know. Formerly the power of Congress in this respect was not so full blown. However, in 1891, *In re Rahrer*[36] sustained the Wilson Act of 1890 which subjected intoxicating liquor to the police power of a state of destination at a point prior to what the Court permitted in the absence of Congressional conditional regulation of the interstate transportation. The serious issue here was that of state constitutional power, to be considered in a later lecture, but the decision may be regarded as a precedent favoring if not wholly establishing the constitutionality of the Federal Lottery Act of 1895 by which Congress absolutely forbade the interstate transportation of {60} lottery tickets, whether the state of destination wanted them excluded or not. This was sustained in 1903 in *Champion v. Ames*, designated by the Reporter *The Lottery Case*.[37]

The issue in the *Lottery* case was clearly deemed a crucial one by the participating Justices. It was first argued in February, 1901, then reargued in October of the same year and again before the full bench in December, 1902. The decision was rendered on February 23, 1903. Mr. Justice Harlan wrote the opinion of the Court, sustaining the conviction for violation of the statute. With him were Justices McKenna, Brown, White, and Holmes. A ten-page dissenting opinion by Mr. Chief Justice Fuller was concurred in by Justices Brewer, Shiras, and Peckham. Although the Court's opinion devoted some space to establishing that "regulation" may in appropriate cases take the form of prohibition, the dissent did not go so far as to deny this *in toto*, but invoked the privileges and immunities clause of Article IV for the assertion "Thus it is seen that the right of passage of persons and property from one State to another cannot be prohibited by Congress."[38]

There is also a vague intimation that the national commercial power, concededly broad and complete over foreign commerce, does not stretch so extensively over interstate commerce, because of the reserved powers of the states. After asserting that a lottery ticket is not an article of commerce and does not become so because put in an envelope and transported, Mr. Chief Justice Fuller continues:

> An invitation to dine, or to take a drive, or a note of introduction, all become articles of commerce under the ruling in this case, by being deposited with an express company for transportation. {61} This in effect breaks down all differences between that which is, and that which is not, an article of commerce, and the necessary consequence is to take from the States all jurisdiction over the subject so far as interstate communication is concerned. It is a long step in the direction of wiping out all traces of state lines, and the creation of a centralized Government.[39]

The Chief Justice also invokes the constitutional prohibition on Congress against laying any tax on articles exported from any state, and, disregarding cases to the contrary, says that it seems to him that "it was plainly intended to apply to interstate transportation as well."[40] With this I would be inclined to agree as an initial ruling according to Marshall, but it does not follow that denial of a ban on transit follows from a denial of power to tax. We shall note later different criteria for the power to tax and the power to suppress. The Chief Justice himself has to recognize sanction for the prohibition of the interstate "transportation of diseased animals and infected goods."[41] These prohibitions, he says, are for the protection of transportation itself, and they are essentially commercial in their nature.

The dissenting Cassandra prophecy of doom to our system from the decision ("as long ago observed, it is with governments as with religions, the form may survive the substance of the faith")[42] did not deter the majority. With presumably the restriction of the due process clause of the Fifth Amendment in mind, Mr. Justice Harlan suggests that "The whole subject is too important, and the questions suggested by its consideration are too difficult of solution, to justify any attempt to lay down a rule for determining in advance {62} the validity of every statute that may be enacted under the commerce clause."[43] There are evils that may flow from lottery tickets. The tickets "are subjects of traffic" and "have a money value in the market."[44] For some unknown reason, not clearly a courageous one, the opinion fails to deal with *Paul v. Virginia*,[45] which held that an insurance policy is not an article of commerce. It would seem that it would have been appropriate to discount in some way reliance of the dissenting opinion on the insurance case. It was to be over forty years before this case suffered desuetude after surviving for three-quarters of a century.

It is not to be assumed that the minority in the *Lottery* case would have invoked the Fourteenth Amendment against suppression of lotteries by a state. It was doubtless the expansion of the exercise of national power that was foremost in their minds. From this standpoint the lottery statute differed from the Erdman Act which was condemned by a vote of six to two in *Adair v. United States*[46] in 1908. The statute, passed in 1898, providing for arbitration of labor disputes on interstate railroads, forbade employers to discharge employees because of their membership in a labor union. After condemning it under the Fifth Amendment as an infringement on liberty of contract, Mr. Justice Harlan declared further that "we hold that there is no such connection between interstate commerce and membership in a labor organization"[47] as to authorize Congress to forbid discharge of union members. This seems to be unreason run riot. In dissenting, Mr. Justice McKenna points out that the Court had held that Congress may "establish a rule of liability of {63} a carrier to employees for personal injuries received in its service," and had sustained the Safety Appliance Act, which he said, "is even more round about in its influence on commerce and as much so as the prohibition"[48] involved in the present case.

One good way to test the Lottery Act and the Erdman Act as regulations of interstate commerce is to focus imaginative attention on similar state statutes applicable to interstate transportation and to union membership of railroad employees. Could there be any doubt that the Court would have regarded such state statutes as regulations of interstate commerce? Conceivably the state might now be permitted to forbid entrance of lottery tickets in spite of the fact that they are regulations of interstate commerce, but this is beside the point, now that states are accorded more self-protective power even against intrusions from without. Nevertheless it is obvious that national regulation uniform throughout the country is to be preferred in dealing with interstate shipments and interstate workers. From the standpoint of enterprise that desires to be let alone, there is of course a greater danger of would-be regulators having to convince only a single legislative body than to secure acquiescence from forty-eight, but if this is a consideration which moved the condemnatory Justices in these two cases, it should be predicated on the Fifth Amendment and not on the contention that interstate commerce was not sufficiently directly involved. And on the Fifth Amendment too, I would deem it illegitimate.

When Congress sets a barrier across the channels of interstate commerce, it interferes with production in the producing {64} state to the extent that such production is dependent on access to an extrastate market. The lottery enterprise then conducted in Louisiana was curtailed by the Anti-Lottery Act sustained by the *Lottery* case. The production of impure foods was curbed when the national Pure Food and Drug Act punished their shipment to sister states. Breweries and distilleries suffered when Congress allowed market states to deal with their products as they dealt with beer and liquor of local origin, and as they did when Congress forbade the interstate transportation of intoxicating liquor designed by any person interested therein to be received, possessed, used, or sold in violation of the law of the state of destination. Yet the Wilson Act and the Webb-Kenyon Act were sustained,[49] notwithstanding their adverse effect on the brewing and distilling in sister states which did not discourage but presumably favored their tax-paying and delight-giving liquefactions.

When before the Constitution our thirteen states were substantially separate and almost independent nations, each state could keep out the products of its neighbors to their consequent disadvantage. After the Constitution got in established working order, the Supreme Court restricted the states from burdening interstate trade and transportation by various forms of taxation and by various police measures. It was because the states were not permitted to have free rein over interstate transportation and over products from sister states that Congress began sporadically and timidly to do what the states were forbidden to do. It might seem that after condemnation of a state law as a regulation of interstate {65} commerce, an identical act of Congress must perforce be sanctioned as a regulation of such commerce and held valid as such unless barred by some other clause such as the Fifth Amendment. This, however, did not always meet with full judicial favor. Four Justices objected in the *Lottery* case and five condemned in the *Child Labor* case.[50]

The condemnatory opinion of Mr. Justice Day in the *Child Labor* case cannot successfully claim to be of the highest intellectual order. It contains a number of statements that in their generality are incontrovertible, but they are often irrelevant or inapposite. Of course Congress may not exercise a power not entrusted to it by the Constitution. Of course the maintenance of the authority of the states over matters essentially local is important. But these and other truisms do not establish that any state ever had a "local power always existing" to say what products its neighbors must receive, or that such receipt by a sister state is a matter "purely local" to North Carolina or is one of its "purely internal affairs."[51] Nowhere does Mr. Justice Day specifically controvert the dissenting observation of Mr. Justice Holmes:

> The Act does not meddle with anything belonging to the States. They may regulate their internal affairs and their domestic commerce as they like. But when they seek to send their product across the state line they are no longer within their rights.[52]

What Mr. Justice Day does is to neglect the analysis of Mr. Justice Holmes and to start on a different track. The reserved power of the state is to him not the power to insist on shipment to other states, but the power to regulate manufacture. {66} But Congress forbade no method of manufacturing. In so far as Mr. Justice Day says the contrary, he is wrong even as to manufacturing to ship to an extrastate market. He commits the all too familiar error of a false dichotomy when he says that "The act in its effect does not regulate transportation among the States, but aims to standardize the ages at which children may be employed in mining and manufacturing within the States."[53] Of course to a partial extent the Act does both. It certainly regulates transportation to the extent that it puts an end to it. It standardizes the ages of working children only to the extent that an employer may desire them to work on products for extra-state consumption. Without doubt the Act discouraged some individuals from doing what their state did not forbid, but it did not, like some exercises of federal power, forbid them to do what their state required.[54] If we were to go into the matter of motive, it may be conceded that Congress by the Act wanted to end child labor so far as Congress has a leverage to discourage it. Very likely Congress would welcome the irony of Sarah Cleghorn's quatrain:

> The golf course lies so near the mill,
> That almost every day
> The laboring children can look out
> And see the men at play.[55]

Mr. Justice Day thinks it important that the textiles from the factories in which these North Carolina children worked {67} were "harmless." This must be taken to mean in legal essence that such harm as was incident to the employment of the North Carolina children was over and done for as soon as the cotton textiles were made and ready for shipment. Congressional dealing with liquor, lottery tickets, and impure food was justified because the transportation brought harm to the states of destination. These textiles were "ordinary commercial commodities."[56] If this is designed to flirt obliquely with a due process restraint, it is erroneous. The due process clause protects "persons." It does not say goods. Persons do not have protection from the state against child labor laws. If they may by proper authority be forbidden to employ, why may they not by proper authority be forbidden to ship the fruits? Even if it were contended that Congress suffers some restraint from some unknown source against forbidding shipments of the fruits of past harm, though not of future harm, the approval of the White Slave Act[57] would negative its acceptance. That Act was more concerned with preventing enticement and kidnapping of women from their home state to concealment and sin in sister states than it was with the locus where the sin might flourish. It was to prevent harm and evil before transportation as much as or more than harm and evil at journey's end.

The harm in child labor took place before shipment. The goods were themselves harmless. The transportation was not the cause of the harm. Such are the postulates somehow extracted from the secret recesses of the commerce clause. To this there are two answers. The transportation, if not a "cause" of the harm in terms of physics, was a *sine qua non* of the harm. Access to markets is essential to manufacture {68} for the intended markets. Secondly, with the incapacity of states of destination to exclude products from other states that are not impure,[58] only Congress may save Massachusetts from competition in Massachusetts and elsewhere throughout the country stemming from factories in states with lower standards of labor legislation. Mr. Justice Day disposes of this by stark assertion:

> There is no power vested in Congress to require the States to exercise their police power so as to prevent possible unfair competition. Many causes may co-operate to give one State, by reason of local laws or conditions, an economic advantage over others. The Commerce Clause was not intended to give to Congress a general authority to equalize such conditions. In some of the States laws have

been passed fixing minimum wages for women; in others the local law regulates the hours of labor of women in various employments. Business done in such States may be at an economic disadvantage when compared with States which have no such regulations; surely, this fact does not give Congress the power to deny transportation in interstate commerce to those who carry on business where the hours of labor and the rate of compensation for women have not been fixed by a standard in use in other States and approved by Congress.[59]

In so far as this was true by judicial fiat, the lot of the nation might be thought to be not wholly a happy one. The only solace we might have had at the moment was that its truth was wholly the product of judicial fiat, and like that of the figure in Selden's *Table Talk*, the product of the Odd Man. True, the power of Congress in such efforts at equalization may be exercised unwisely, but the courts profess that issues of wisdom are not for them to consider. Undoubtedly {69} in Mr. Justice Day's breast there was a fear of what Congress might go on to do if the authority exercised in the Child Labor Law were sanctioned. This finds expression in his concluding paragraph:

> The far-reaching result of upholding the Act cannot be more plainly indicated than by pointing out that if Congress can thus regulate matters entrusted to local authority by prohibition of the movement of commodities in interstate commerce, all freedom of commerce may be at an end, and the power of the States over local matters may be eliminated, and thus our system of government be practically destroyed.[60]

This apparently is where in substance we have now arrived in 1955. Nevertheless God reigns as much as ever and the Republic still lives.

True enough, the sanction of the power exerted in the Child Labor Law would make a significant change in our polity, as the overruling of the *Child Labor* case now has done.[61] But the change is not so complete as Mr. Justice Day thought possible. The prescriptions of the Child Labor Law deal with local matters only in so far as they feed on interstate transportation. There was an adequate nexus between the transportation and the conditions annexed to its lawfulness and unlawfulness. The now valid successor of the Child Labor Law could not in my judgment go so far as to forbid transportation of persons or property from a state where there is a poll tax requirement for voting, where the expenditure for schools is less than at a prescribed rate, where the age of consent is less than eighteen, where divorces are granted on a residence or pretended domicile of so short a period as six weeks, or where many other conditions {70} are picked that have no dependence on transportation.

Possibly Mr. Justice Day's apprehension of the validity of a wider progeny of Congressional exertions if he had been the odd man on the other side of the constitutional fence was encouraged by a dissenting argument of Mr. Justice Holmes. After saying that when the states "seek to send their products across the state line they are no longer within their rights," Holmes went on:

> If there were no Constitution and no Congress their power to cross the line would depend upon their neighbors. Under the Constitution such commerce belongs not to the States but to Congress to regulate. It may carry out its views of public policy whatever indirect effect they may have upon the activities of the States. Instead of being encountered by a prohibitive tariff at her boundaries the State encounters the public policy of the United States which it is for Congress to express. The public policy of the United States is shaped with a view to the benefit of the nation as a whole. . . . The national welfare as understood by Congress may require a different attitude within its sphere from that of some self-seeking State. It seems to me entirely constitutional for Congress to enforce its understanding by all the means at its command.[62]

This seems to set no limits to the conditions that Congress may make the determining factor in permitting and forbidding transportation. Unfortunately, as it seems to me, Mr. Justice Stone in the *Darby* case which sanctioned the Fair Labor Standards Act and overruled the *Dagenhart* case referred to "the powerful and now classic dissent of Mr. Justice Holmes"[63] in the earlier case, without any specific {71} caveat as to the conditions that may be annexed to the prohibition.

It is not to be assumed, however, that either of these distinguished Justices had in mind the possibility of Congressional efforts to suppress any local conduct wholly unrelated to and disconnected from at least the possibility of interstate transportation. In dealing with the section of the Wages and Hours Act which directly regulates the rates of pay and the standard work day, Mr. Justice Stone notes that what the statute deals with is wages and hours of employees engaged in the production of goods for interstate commerce, and that the prohibitions on interstate shipment are of goods manufactured by employees whose wages and hours violate the direct federal regulation of them. So there is no warrant for assuming that any of the Justices intended to give to Congress all the power that states possessed under the Articles of Confederation or all the powers that Congress may have over foreign commerce. Mr. Justice Stone, however, is very latitudinarian in suggesting the scope of production for interstate commerce.

When the Wages and Hours Act says "commerce," it means by prior definition the type of commerce within direct national regulatory power, thus avoiding repetition of the words foreign, Indian, and among the several states. The *Darby* opinion expands this well nigh to the limit by saying that it includes production of goods which the employer according to the normal course of his business intends or expects to move in interstate commerce. In the *Kirschbaum* case,[64] the engineers, electricians, elevator operators, {72} and the like were held to be engaged in the production of goods for commerce because the tenants of the loft building which they served were engaged in the production of goods for commerce. The manufacturers could not produce for commerce without having a building to produce in. The building would not serve the tenants unless it were so served as to be serviceable. Such was the house-that-Jack-built construction. Even more remote from actual production for commerce were the diggers of oil wells, because there were thought to be reasonable grounds for anticipation that the oil later produced would to a large extent be shipped in interstate commerce.[65] These interpretations were of a provision which referred to production and did not mention shipment.

The Wages and Hours Act also deals with child labor, by prohibiting the shipment in interstate commerce of goods produced in an establishment employing children under the prescribed age. If a water boy of tender years, in obedience to the cup-of-cold-water command of the Scriptures, solaced the drillers for oil when they were thirsty, could the oil be denied an outlet to a sister state because he was underpaid or too young to be employed at all? Fantastic as might seem an affirmative answer to such fantastic questions, there were together at one period four Justices of the Supreme Court who very likely could have been persuaded by their kindly hearts to stretch the statute to such extent. These four were the ones who voted that the messenger boys of the Western Union are engaged in the production of goods for commerce.[66] To indulge in such a conclusion, {73} it was necessary to opine that telegrams are "goods," that the messenger boys are engaged in their "production," and that the Western Union later "ships" the telegrams. Mr. Chief Justice Stone and Justices Roberts, Reed, Frankfurter, and Jackson thought that these intermediate steps were too tenuous for them to take, even to do good, if good it would be.

The Wages and Hours Act applies to those "in commerce" as well as to those in "production for commerce." This brings up bothersome questions of whether the interstate phase of transit has ended and local hauling has begun. A wholesaler orders goods from an extrastate manufacturer and after receiving them delivers them to his retail customers. Does this constitute two journeys or only one? Does it matter whether the wholesaler orders in order to fill an order already received or whether he merely is confident that he will get an order if he can get the goods in advance to fill it? These are not tremendously fascinating or exciting issues to challenge the constitutional acuteness of nine lawyers in a lofty judicial role, but they are issues that have to be resolved, some one way, and others another. They resemble the questions that formerly had to be answered under the Federal Employers' Liability Act in order to inform the administratrix whether her husband was killed in the course of interstate commerce or not. They resemble the questions whether commodities are in "transit" or have stopped for an "independent local advantage" so as to be subject to state property taxation. There are vagaries and varieties in the answers that such questions have met.

Before the Federal Employers' Liability Act was amended to broaden its coverage, it applied only when the person {74} suffering the injury was employed in interstate commerce at the time of his injury. Coaling and oiling an engine in the roundhouse at the end of a trip to get it ready to start soon on its next one brought the injured employee under the statute.[67] Overhauling the engine in the shops took it out of commerce for the time being.[68] It was once held that a cook cooking for a crew mending a bridge bearing tracks over which interstate trains ran was in interstate commerce, though cooking is not commerce at all, in and of itself. This went so far that the Court had to expand its formula to cover one in interstate commerce "or in work so closely connected therewith as to be substantially a part thereof."[69] But later this case was criticized and perhaps overruled.[70] At any rate the Court refused to follow it far enough to apply the Wages and Hours Act to a cook cooking for a caterer with a contract to feed railroad employees in a mobile dining car belonging to the railroad.[71] Four Justices dissented, and it is hardly necessary to point out who they were. It should be noted that Mr. Justice Reed for the majority is talking, not constitutional law, but only statutory interpretation. He says that Congress did not intend the coverage to go to the utmost reaches of constitutional power, and notes that, unlike the Wagner Act, the Wages and Hours Act does not refer to labor "affecting commerce" but to labor "in commerce" or "in production of goods for commerce." "There is," he adds, "no single concept of inter-state {75} commerce that can be applied to every federal statute regulating commerce."[72]

This type of thinking is similar to what goes on in presumably technical constitutional law, though the results are not the same. From the standpoint of state taxation, goods are still in "interstate transit" though they are immobile, provided they stop only because the transportation facilities require it. They are out of transit if they stop for what is called an "independent local advantage," like taking grain from the cars to an elevator to be cleaned, graded, and weighed before resuming its journey to its ultimate destination.[73] A shepherd once led his sheep across a second state into a third. He led them by still waters and by green pastures, and they weighed more when they arrived at the stockyards than when they had been at home on the range. The question was whether they were going to feed or just feeding to go. The Supreme Court thought that they were just feeding to go and so held them immune from taxation in the intermediate state.[74] Cases of this type once took me four articles in a law review to consider in detail.[75]

Although the Supreme Court decisions denying application of the Wages and Hours Act and the Wagner Act to occasional situations may be confined to statutory interpretation, the subjection of defendants to the legislative and administrative toils has to be constitutional law. Moreover if the cases condemning the Guffey Coal Act, the Child Labor Act, the Railway Pension Act, and the National Industrial {76} Recovery Act[76] had remained law, and the pre-1937 bench had survived till 1940, these later labor statutes would undoubtedly have similarly found their way to the judicial wastebasket. What Mr. Justice Day so curtly dismissed in his Child Labor opinion, Mr. Justice Stone makes the basis of the national power to go beyond commerce and deal with relations between employer and employed in production.[77] He agrees that production is not commerce and hence cannot be interstate commerce. He escapes from the force of this by saying that "it does not follow that Congress may not by appropriate legislation regulate intrastate activities where they have a substantial effect on interstate commerce."[78] This sufficiently substantial effect of substandard wages on interstate commerce was found through the force of competition between different factories for the same markets. Substandard wages in one state will tend to force wages in other states to the same level. Every good Republican who favors protective tariffs ought to know this. Manufacturers have often been familiar with it when it worked to their advantage or disadvantage. Yet the majority in the first Child Labor case failed to recognize it. Now after a life of twenty-three years, that mistaken case received a well deserved repose.

The *Darby* opinion, sustaining the Wages and Hours Act, was handed down on February 3, 1941. The decision was {77} unanimous, Mr. Justice McReynolds having retired two days earlier. The Wagner Act was sustained in 1937 in *N.L.R.B. v. Jones and Laughlin Steel Corp.* and companion cases.[79] It was not unanimous. Mr. Justice McReynolds wrote a long dissent in which Justices Van Devanter, Sutherland, and Butler joined. The opinion of the Court by Mr. Chief Justice Hughes was somewhat along the line of his *Shreveport* opinion in his earlier judicial incarnation.[80] There he said that the relation between intrastate rates and interstate rates is "as a relation" within the power of the nation to deal with. Here he affirms that dangers to interstate commerce may come from outside of commerce, citing Sherman Law precedents. Interferences by employers with union organization and union activity may cause widespread interruptions of commerce. The impact of resulting industrial struggles may have a more direct effect on commerce than the Industrial Recovery Act had on the wages and other industrial relations of the Schechter schoctim in preparing poultry from Iowa in a Brooklyn abattoir for the local market. Without detailed analysis Mr. Chief Justice Hughes says that "to find 'immediacy or directness'" in the *Schechter* case would be to find it "'almost everywhere,' a result inconsistent with the maintenance of our Federal system."[81] Of the *Carter Coal* case condemning the Bituminous Coal Conservation Act of 1935, he states briefly what the Court there thought, and says that the *Carter* case and the *Schechter* case "are not controlling here."[82]

Of the due process issue in the case, in view of the *Adair* {78} and the *Coppage* cases,[83] this is not the chapter for comment. The Chief Justice hacked out a distinction by sheer force as he had done earlier in applying the Railroad Labor Act.[84] It could hardly deceive any expert observer. But these two cases clearly annul Mr. Justice Harlan's absurd commerce clause point in the *Adair* case. It would seem, too, that they cast a great shadow on Mr. Justice Roberts's declaration in the *Railway Pension* case[85] that it is not a regulation of commerce to compel an interstate carrier to pay a pension to a retired worker. One of the reasons given by Mr. Justice Van Devanter to sustain the second Employers' Liability Act[86] was that the kindlier rules of liability for injuries to railroad workers were an aid to transportation. From this or from somewhere else Mr. Justice Roberts derives the negative pregnant that a statute that is not an aid to transportation is not a regulation of commerce. Old age of employees is not a responsibility of the employer. He does not cause it. It aids transportation to separate an elderly worker from the service but not to pay him a pension when he toils not, neither does he spin. For the minority of four, Mr. Chief Justice Hughes not only rejects the idea that assurance of a pension is not an aid to transportation, but insists more broadly that it is a regulation of transportation to impose responsibility on the carriers.

In sustaining the Wagner Act in 1937, Mr. Chief Justice Hughes invokes various applications of the Sherman Act that {79} activities outside of commerce may come within the statute because of their effect on commerce. In the antitrust cases, issues of statutory construction are not infrequently so intermingled with constitutional law that it is sometimes not easy to disentangle them. Whichever they are in any given case, the judicial treatment suggests persuasively that the treatment comes from the judges without clear direction from either statute or Constitution. For the judges who have differed in case after case and for those of us who have struggled in vain to find a clear pattern in the jumble of decisions, it hardly enhances self-esteem to learn from Mr. Justice Holmes that the statute is not too indefinite to afford a constitutional basis for criminal prosecution.[87] It is perhaps more comforting to learn from the same writer that "A word is not a crystal, transparent and unchanged, it is the skin of a living thought and may vary greatly in color and content according to the circumstances and the time in which it is used."[88] To which, some one might be tempted to add: "according to the one who is using it or defining it."

It was of course not difficult to distinguish the issue in the *Wagner* case from that in the *Schechter* condemnation of the Industrial Recovery Act. This *Schechter* condemnation was unanimous, so the result is immune from criticism, though it was not necessary to consider the commerce point after administering the hemlock of excessive delegation. It certainly was delegation run riot. On the commerce issue, the Chief Justice invoked the formula applied to deal with state police and taxing measures challenged as in conflict with the commerce clause, *i.e.,* that the state may affect {80} commerce indirectly but not directly. So, he declared, Congress may regulate local matters that affect commerce directly but not those that affect commerce only indirectly. The effect of the Recovery Act on the Schechters and their schoctim was held to be indirect, because if it were held to be direct there would be little state constitutional autonomy left. In short, the regulation went too far. This is supported by the customary parade of imaginary horribles in similar cases. Wages and hours and the mode of selecting chickens from a coop may affect cost and so price, but so do rent and the cost of knives. We might relish more detailed consideration, but there may have been wisdom in restraint. What should have been clear enough at the time was that the application of the statute here was to local practices after the interstate transportation was completed, with no future extrastate effect to follow. After the decision, one of the participating Justices, not unknown to the Columbia Law School, told me that the Recovery Act was no better enforced than was national prohibition. The Blue Eagle did more screaming than effectuating. The President should have been grateful for its slaughter twenty days before its Congressionally decreed demise and perhaps refrained from saying that the Court had taken us back to the horse and buggy days.

Though Mr. Chief Justice Hughes gave satisfactory support for the constitutionality of the Wagner Act, he failed to convince four of his colleagues. The last one of the dissenters retired on February 1, 1941, so that the Wages and Hours Act passed muster without dissent. By the beginning of the 1942 term Mr. Justice Roberts was the only member of the Court not appointed or promoted by President Roosevelt. He too retired in 1945 after the close of the {81} October, 1944, term. The thesis which underlies the title of this series of lectures could be amply supported by the kaleidoscopic voting of Mr. Justice Roberts during his judicial career. He saw a somewhat flickering white light on the road to Damascus after the election of 1936[89] and before the proposal of the so-called Court

Plan of 1937. The light grew stronger and steadier later. Yet in his last two terms he was in dissent in 93 of the 181 cases in which the court was divided. In one third of the dissents he was alone. Of the 62 dissents in which he had companions, they lined up as follows: Mr. Justice Frankfurter, 34 cases; Mr. Chief Justice Stone, 32 cases; Mr. Justice Reed and Mr. Justice Jackson, 19 cases each. With these four colleagues there were 14 agreements in dissent; with Justices Rutledge, Murphy, Douglas, and Black only 11 altogether. Mr. Justice Roberts sanctioned most of the Congressional statutes that were sufficiently specific. His objections were confined largely to the judicial stretching of statutes and the departure from precedents {82} with the consequent uncertainty of the law. In many of these he was in my judgment well justified.

Thus in these two periods before and after 1937, not only was the court divided against itself, but, considering his full fifteen years of judicial service, Mr. Justice Roberts might be said to have been divided against himself. The diversions and the divisions of this fifteen-year period cannot be fully understood without assessment of personalities and regard for the calendar. Four of the Roosevelt appointees were as determined in *their* direction, as four of their predecessors were determined by attraction to the opposite pole. This resembles an earlier period in which on many important issues, White, Van Devanter, and McReynolds were certain to disagree with Holmes, Brandeis, and Clarke, and the decision depended upon which side was favored by two or three of Day, McKenna, and Pitney. Still earlier there was the Field wing and the Miller wing. I once kept score of the two terms from October, 1941, to June, 1943, in which there were 137 split decisions. Mr. Justice Black had 46 dissents, in not one of which was he joined by Mr. Justice Frankfurter. The latter had 40 dissents, in not one of which was he joined by the former. In divided cases in which they both sat, they differed as dissenters 83 times, and were together in the majority 48 times. In 31 of these 48 cases, Mr. Justice Roberts was one or all of the dissenters.

Mr. Justice Roberts wrote the opinion in the *Butler* case[90] which condemned the Agricultural Adjustment Act. Congress imposed a processing tax and used the proceeds to bribe farmers to reduce the number of their acres devoted to various crops. The opinion conceded that the national {83} spending power may achieve results not embraced within the national regulatory powers, but then condemned the donations for idle acres because it achieved results that Congress could not command. William Graham Sumner once said that you can get out of a major premise all that you put into it; but Mr. Justice Roberts drew from a major premise what he had expressly excluded from it. After this rebuff, Congress tried again with the commerce power, as after the rebuff for using the commerce power to pay pensions to railroad workers, it tried again with the taxing and spending powers. Both of these reverse shifts were successful.[91] In *Mulford v. Smith*, Mr. Justice Roberts said that the tobacco regulation does not purport to deal with production; but since it would be foolish for a grower of tobacco to grow more than he is permitted to market, the effect of the statute on production was not for a wise man so very indirect.

The revised crop restriction plan for wheat established quotas after a referendum and penalized production in excess of the quota. This was sustained in *Wickard v.Filburn*[92] in an able latitudinarian opinion by Mr. Justice Jackson. This abandoned the adjectives and nouns previously bandied about in the opinions and planted itself on practical economic considerations of the effect of crop restriction on prices. "Direct," "indirect," "production," "consumption," "marketing" were terms thrown into the discard so far as the scope of national power is concerned, though they may be helpful in some cases of statutory interpretation. In summary Mr. Justice Jackson says that ". . . even if appellee's activity be local and though it may not be regarded as {84} commerce, it may still, whatever its nature, be reached by Congress if it exerts a substantial economic effect on interstate commerce, and this irrespective of whether such effect is what might at some earlier time have been defined as 'direct' or 'indirect.'"[93] And this he regards as a return to Mr. Chief Justice Marshall. The reach of the judgment in the particular case is made clear by its application to all grain grown on the farm in excess of the quota, including that consumed on the farm for feeding the grower's own stock. Obviously the crop restriction plan could in considerable or in large measure be restricted or defeated if grain grown for home consumption may not be included in the allowable quota. With this opinion by a much lamented Justice, formalism has been succeeded by plain common sense.

Here endeth the lesson of the vagaries and variations of Supreme Court decisions and opinions on the scope of Congressional power over interstate commerce. There are other important illustrations of similar exhibitions, but it is believed that they would not significantly change the picture. Not all of the Justices who have participated in weaving this intellectual and political tapestry have been of equal intellectual acumen and wisdom. Those who have been for keeping the national power within narrow limits have undoubtedly been from time to time firmly imbued with a *laissez faire* doctrine, and some presumably have been sincerely seeking to think what the Framers and the Ratifiers would have thought in the late eighteenth century. Happily, however, the Framers were wise enough in their day to leave room for the judgments of their successors, though they {85}could not anticipate the economic and physical integration that would make all sections of the continent from sea to sea members one of another. The infant nation was fortunate to have a Washington, a Hamilton, and a Marshall to start it on its way. And latterly it has been fortunate to have judicial successors to Marshall who have been aware that a nation should have the power of a nation. Whether Congress can always with wisdom wield the wide powers now accorded to it, is a different matter.

Without advance design I have more than filled my time with consideration of commerce complexities, though my title was broad enough to cover other national powers as well. By way of justification, it may be suggested that an abundance of detail of the judicial handling of a single topic may give a clearer picture of methods and results than would be presented by a more cursory survey of a wider territory. This, however, may be just an excuse for an unintentional inadvertence. But certainly the commerce powers of the nation and the states raise the most perennial and persistent problems of constitutional federalism. Now the states are authoritatively recognized as possessed of a commerce power. They have powers of police and of taxation that raise commerce clause issues to be dealt with in later lectures. Once it was thought that the test of what states may do is what the nation may not do, or that the test of what the states may not do is what the nation may do, but the criteria are no longer so clear cut as that. The involutions of state power must be considered with a greater particularity than can be compressed into a formula.

From one standpoint the war power of the nation may be deemed of transcending importance, as indeed it is. But the {86} tolerance of the Supreme Court toward purported exercises of the war power has been such that there is little question as to its constitutional scope. National powers over money and banking have not since Marshall's day raised great conflicts as to what national banks may be authorized to do. Quite otherwise is the power over the currency. The first *Legal Tender* cases and their subsequent reversal[94] after a change in the personnel of the Supreme Court have been fruitful illustrations of diversity in judiciality. Congressional annulment of gold clauses in private securities and abrogation of the gold promise in public securities[95] may well invite careful scrutiny of arguments and dispositions, but these issues are sporadic and exceptional. Yet how it could be held that Congress may not renege on a national promise to pay in gold of specified density, and then apply to the bondholder the tort measure of damages instead of the contract one, well nigh passes comprehension. Only Mr. Justice Stone of the majority found the appropriate way to reach the well-nigh necessary result. The minority of course accepted the necessity of choosing between him and Mr. Chief Justice Hughes.

The taxing power would require a treatise to elucidate its ramifications, as indeed it receives in these latter days. Supposedly it may not be used to suppress an enterprise if the Supreme Court can catch on to what it is up to, as it failed to do in the case of the ten-cents-a-pound tax on oleomargarine colored to resemble butter,[96] as butter resembles {87} butter. An extra 10 percent tax on the income of employers of designated children fell by the wayside as patently suppressive.[97] Hardly candid have been the opinions sanctioning excises on dispensing drugs,[98] on sawed-off machine guns,[99] on engaging in book-making[100] (not publishing), and perhaps on some other enterprise that Congress thought needed watching. The greater quarrels have been over what is a direct tax and what after the Sixteenth Amendment is income. The words of the Constitution and of the Amendment do not give the answers. The Supreme Court gives them, and it has by no means always been consistent or unanimous. Much of this is not so much announcing constitutional formulae as expressing judgments on the characteristics of the practical situation calling for judicial ministration. In this it resembles other applications of constitutional criteria, if criteria they be.

Notes

1 4 Wheat. 316 (1819).

2 9 Wheat. 1 (1824).

3 9 Wheat, at 186.

4 *Id.* at 194.

5 *Id.* at 197.

6 *Ibid.*

7 9 Wheat, at 209.

8 *Id.* at 199.

9 *Ibid.*

10 9 Wheat. at 191.

11 *Id.* at 202-3.

12 U.S. CONST., ART. I, § 9.

13 12 Wheat. 419 (1827).

14 *Id.* at 448.

15 228 U.S. 115.

16 4 Wheat. at 407.

17 *Ibid.*

18 *Ibid.*

19 4 Wheat, at 421.

20 U.S. CONST., ART. I, § 10; 4 Wheat. at 414.

21 Pennsylvania v. Wheeling & Belmont Bridge Co., 18 How. 421.

22 13 How. 518 (1852).

23 United States v. Holliday, 3 Wall. 407.

24 *The Daniel Ball*, 10 Wall. 557.

25 South Carolina v. Georgia, 93 U.S. 4.

26 Sherlock v. Ailing, 93 U.S. 99, 104.

27 Pensacola Tel. Co. v. Western Union Tel. Co., 96 U.S. 1.

28 Cooley v. Board of Wardens of the Port of Philadelphia, 12 How. 299.

29 100 U.S. 82.

30 91 U.S. 275 (1876).

31 91 U.S. at 282.

32 United States v. Trans-Missouri Freight Assn., 166 U.S. 290 (1897); Nash v. United States, 229 U.S. 373 (1913).

33 Interstate Commerce Comm'n. v. Brimson, 154 U.S. 447 (1894).

34 United States v. E. C. Knight Co., 156 U.S. 1 (1895).

35 Swift & Co. v. United States, 196 U.S. 375 (1905).

36 140 U.S. 545.

37 188 U.S. 321 (1903).

38 *Id.* at 374.

39 *Id.* at 371.

40 *Id.* at 373.

41 *Id.* at 374.

42 *Id.* at 375.

43 *Id.* at 363.

44 *Id.* at 354.

45 8 Wall. 168 (1869).

46 208 U.S. 161.

47 *Id.* at 179.

48 *Id.* at 189.

49 *In re* Rahrer, 140 U.S. 545 (1891); Clark Distilling Co. v. Western Md. Ry., 242 U.S. 311 (1917).

50 Hammer v. Dagenhart, 247 U.S. 251 (1918).

51 *Id.* at 274, 275.

52 *Id.* at 281.

53 *Id.* at 271-72,

54 E.g., McDermott v. Wisconsin, 228 U.S. 115 (1913) (labeling under Food and Drug Act); Houston, E. & W. Tex. Ry. v. United States, 234 U.S. 342 (1914) (freight rates under Interstate Commerce Act).

55 Published in The Conning Tower, New York Herald Tribune, Jan. 23, 1915.

56 247 U.S. at 276.

57 Hoke v. United States, 227 U.S. 308 (1913).

58 Leisy v. Hardin, 135 U.S. 100 (1890); Schollenberger v. Pennsylvania, 171 U.S. 1 (1898); cf. Crossman v. Lurman, 192 U.S. 189 (1904).

59 247 U.S. at 273.

60 Id. at 276.

61 United States v. Darby, 312 U.S. 100 (1941).

62 247 U.S. at 281.

63 United States v. Darby, 312 U.S. 100, 115 (1941).

64 A. B. Kirschbaum Co. v. Walling, 316 U.S. 517 (1942).

65 Warren-Bradshaw Co. v. Hall, 317 U.S. 88 (1942).

66 Western Union Tel. Co. v. Lenroot, 323 U.S. 490 (1945).

67 New York Cent. R.R. v. Marcone, 281 U.S. 345 (1930).

68 Shanks v. Delaware, L. & W. R.R., 239 U.S. 556 (1916).

69 Philadelphia, B. & W. R.R. v. Smith, 250 U.S. 101 (1919).

70 New York, N.H. & H. R.R. v. Bezue, 284 U.S. 415 (1932), and cases there cited.

71 McLeod v. Threlkeld, 319 U.S. 491 (1943).

72 Id. at 495.

73 Bacon v. Illinois, 227 U.S. 504 (1913).

74 Kelley v. Rhoads, 188 U.S. 1 (1903).

75 Taxation of Things in Transit, 7 VA. L. REV. 167, 245, 429, 497 (1920, 1921).

76 Carter v. Carter Coal Co., 298 U.S. 238 (1936); Hammer v. Dagenhart, 247 U.S. 251 (1918); Railroad Retirement Bd. v. Alton R.R., 295 U.S. 330 (1935); Schechter Poultry Corp. v. United States, 295 U.S. 495 (1935).

77 United States v. Darby, 312 U.S. 100 (1941), sustaining the Fair Labor Standards Act.

78 312 U.S. at 119.

79 301 U.S. 1.

80 Houston, E. & W. Tex. Ry. v. United States, supra n. 54.

81 301 U.S. at 40-41.

82 Id. at 41.

83 Adair v. United States, 208 U.S. 161 (1908); Coppage v. Kansas, 236 U.S. 1 (1915).

84 Texas & N. O. R.R. v. Brotherhood of Ry. Clerks, 281 U.S. 548 (1930).

85 Supra n. 76.

86 Mondou v. New York, N. H. & H. R.R., 223 U.S. 1 (1912).

87 Nash v. United States, 229 U.S. 373 (1913).

88 Towne v. Eisner, 245 U.S. 418, 425 (1918).

89 In Associated Industries v. Department of Labor, 299 U.S. 515, decided November 23, 1936, involving the validity of the New York unemployment insurance law, the Court was equally divided, Mr. Justice Stone not participating; presumably Mr. Justice Roberts voted with Chief Justice Hughes and Justices Brandeis and Cardozo. In West Coast Hotel Co. v. Parrish, 300 U.S. 379 (1937), where Mr. Justice Roberts voted to sustain the Washington minimum-wage law despite his vote with the majority in the *Tipaldo* case, less than a year earlier, condemning the New York minimum-wage law, the decision was reached in late December, 1936. See 2 PUSEY, CHARLES EVANS HUGHES 757 (1951). It should be observed that in the *Tipaldo* case the dissent of Chief Justice Hughes endeavored to distinguish the precedent of Adkins v. Children's Hospital, 261 U.S. 525 (1923), while in the *West Coast Hotel* case the Chief Justice's majority opinion overruled the *Adkins*case. In *Tipaldo,* moreover, counsel for the state did not ask that *Adkins* be overruled. Thus Mr. Justice Roberts's position in the two cases can be harmonized as the view of one who was unable to distinguish the *Adkins* case but who would accept an opportunity to overrule it.

90 United States v. Butler, 297 U.S. 1 (1936).

91 *Supra* chap. ii, n. 39.

92 *Ibid.*

93 317 U.S. at 125.

94 Hepburn v. Griswold, 8 Wall. 603 (1869); Legal Tender Cases, 12 Wall. 457 (1871).

95 Norman v. Baltimore & Ohio R.R., 294 U.S. 240 (1935); Perry v. United States, 294 U.S. 330 (1935).

96 McCray v. United States, 195 U.S. 27 (1904).

97 Child Labor Tax Case, 259 U.S. 20 (1922).

98 United States v. Doremus, 249 U.S. 86; United States v. Sanchez, 340 U.S. 42 (1950).

99 Sonzinsky v. United States, 300 U.S. 506 (1937).

100 United States v. Kahriger, 345 U.S. 22 (1953).

IV. Federalism: Intergovernmental Relations

IT IS HARD to find the clause of the Constitution on which Marshall bases his decision in *M'Culloch v. Maryland*[1] that a state may not impose a stamp tax on notes issued by the Bank of the United States. It is hard to find, because it is not there. There is no such clause. Marshall knew this, but it did not stand in his way. For he says:

> There is no express provision for the case, but the claim has been sustained on a principle which so entirely pervades the constitution, is so intermixed with the materials which compose it, so interwoven with its web, so blended with its texture, as to be incapable of being separated from it, without rending it into shreds.[2]

This is good literature, and by the force of judicial power, it has become good law, subject to variations and vagaries. The "great principle" is put as follows:

> . . . that the constitution and the laws made in pursuance thereof are supreme; that they control the constitution and laws of the respective States, and cannot be controlled by them. From this, which may be almost termed an axiom, other propositions are deduced as corollaries. . . . These are, 1st. that a power to create implies a power to preserve. 2nd. That a power to destroy, if wielded by a different hand, is hostile to, and incompatible with these powers to create and to preserve. 3d. That where this repugnancy exists, that authority which is supreme must control, not yield to that over which it is supreme.[3]

{89} These postulates, if accepted, would afford a sufficient foundation on which to sanction an act of Congress prohibiting deleterious state taxation of national instrumentalities. But this was not enough for Marshall. There was no such act of Congress. So the opinion proceeds to the realm of political theory: "If we measure the power of taxation residing in a State, by the extent of sovereignty which the people of a single State possess, and can confer on its government, we have an intelligible standard, applicable to every case to which the power may be applied."[4] Find the limits of sovereignty, and all difficulties are at an end. Sovereignty is the intelligible standard applicable to every case. If it were really so easy as Marshall professes to think, the most merciful of critics could hardly condone the wanderings of his successors in the path he initiated. There is, however, another approach to the problem. Find out from judicial decisions or otherwise what the states may do and may not do, and we may mark the scope and limits of their sovereignty.

Marshall's arguments are masterly but not impeccable, and, not infrequently, they go too far. He has a conception that anything created by the nation, though within the territorial borders of a state, is beyond, outside of, or above the purview of state power to touch. Beyond extra-territoriality, he imposes a concept of something we may call extra-sovereignality. If the states may tax one instrumentality of the nation, they may tax all: the mail, the mint, patent rights, the papers in the customhouse, judicial process. If they may tax a little, they may tax a lot. If they may not tax a lot, they may not tax a little. The power to tax is the {90} power to destroy. If the states may destroy by taxation, they may destroy by police proscriptions. How simple all this is. If only it were true and had remained so, we who have been concerned with the issues would have been spared a lot. I might not need to make intergovernmental immunities the subject of a lecture. Of course there might be subordinate difficulties of application. Should you look only to the enterprise or activity or person or object that the state designates as the subject of the tax, or should you go beyond names to economics and condemn if a tax on a proper subject is measured in ways that take toll from exercises of national power even by means that may for lack of clarity be called indirect?

Marshall in the actual and precise matter before him was not faced by such problems. Here Maryland by a stamp tax on notes issued by the Bank of the United States was directly hitting the exercise of a function of the Bank. Still more narrowly, which Marshall forbore to consider, the state tax was confined to notes issued by banks not chartered by the state of Maryland. The only such bank in Maryland was the Bank of the United States. The power to tax may not be the power to destroy if the tax is general in application, but the power to impose an adversely discriminatory tax is certainly the power to destroy, if we accept Marshall's dictum in *Brown v. Maryland*[5] that "Questions of power do not depend on the degree to which it may be exercised."[6] A power to tax is not necessarily a power to prohibit, but a power to impose an unlimited adversely discriminatory tax may be exercised so as to suppress.

The Bank of the United States was a somewhat mongrel institution with ownership of stock divided between the {91} United States and private persons. The functions of issuing currency and of engaging in various other undertakings were national public functions. The function of note issue was all that was held to be immune. Marshall with his instinct for making distinctions, sometimes exercised and sometimes not, here conceded that the states may tax the real estate of the bank along with other real property, and may tax the interest of private persons in the bank, along with other similar property. There were no such private interests in the post office or the mint. A further argument in the opinion is open to question. This is that the immunity accorded by the decision "does not deprive the States of any resources which they originally possessed."[7] The thought seems to be that originally there were no national enterprises to be taxed, for none existed. The weakness here is that to the extent that the national creation supersedes prior state-created and privately initiated undertakings, the state is fiscally worse off than it was previously.

Marshall declined to invoke on behalf of his ruling a reciprocal relationship between state and nation. In answer to a contention that an argument that would sustain national taxation of state banks would similarly sustain state taxation of national banks, he said that "the two cases are not on the same reason."[8] The nation is the government of all. When the nation taxes, it acts on its own constituents. When the states tax national institutions they act

> upon the measures of a government created by others as well as themselves, for the benefit of others in common with themselves. The difference is that which always exists, and always must exist, between the action of the whole on a part, and the action of a part on the whole—between the laws of a government {92} declared to be supreme, and those of a government which, when in opposition to those laws, is not supreme.[9]

Thus does Marshall cleverly make use of an argument in favor of equal power in nation and state, not only to deny state power but also to deny state immunity from national power. He adds that if the argument denies the power of Congress to tax state banks, it would not "prove the right of the States to tax the Bank of the United States."[10] The question whether there is reciprocity between the taxing powers of state and nation and the immunity of each from the power of the other remained unsettled for over fifty years.[11] It was not determined in *Veazie Bank v. Fenno*[12] in 1869, which sanctioned a national excise of 10 percent on notes issued by state banks to circulate as money, because it was there held that Congress with its power over the circulating medium might directly forbid the issue of such state notes. Justices Nelson and Davis dissented.

Marshall has one more bite of the cherry of national immunity in *Weston v. City of Charleston*[13] in 1829. This condemns a state tax on the capital value of what we would now call bonds of the United States in the hands of individual and corporate owners. The effect of the tax, says Marshall, is to act on the power of the nation to borrow money, before it is exercised. He does not observe that to some extent the tax was discriminatory because it did not apply to all property. Justices Johnson and Thompson dissented, being of the opinion that the tax was on income and a general tax on all incomes, which seems hard to accept from the terms of the statute. The dissent, whether justified {93} on this assumption or not, is, however, significant as showing that two of the Justices would distinguish between a tax on capital and a tax on income, a distinction the Court later rejected. The difference may not have been so material in 1829 as it became later, for the tax was on "six and seven per cent stock of the United States." But when the United States can borrow at 3 percent and private borrowers may have to pay 6 percent, a 2-percent tax on capital will take two thirds of the income from a United States bond and one third of the income on private securities, except as modified by other factors.

The *Weston* case was followed in two cases in 1863 in which a New York tax on the capital of state chartered banks was held to be imposed on their property and therefore on United States bonds to the extent that their capital was invested in them.[14] This differed from the tax on selected kinds of property condemned in the *Weston*case, because discrimination against any particular species of property was avoided, when all investments and assets were included in capital and surplus. This did not matter, says Mr. Justice Nelson. The objection in the Weston case was not discrimination but subjection. After the 1863 adverse decisions, New York changed its statute to impose the tax on banks "on a valuation equal to the amount of their capital stock paid in, or secured to be paid in, and their surplus earnings . . .";[15] but this did not fool the Supreme Court. Again the United States bonds had to be deducted from the appraisal.[16] But in a concluding sentence Mr. Justice {94} Nelson foreshadows a future distinction when he remarks that he has examined the New York statutes taxing moneyed corporations from 1823 to date, and notes that "it will be seen in all of them that the tax is imposed on the property of the institutions, as contra-distinguished from a tax upon their privileges or franchises."[17]

Three years later this distinction became the ground for sustaining in full a series of state taxes when these taxes were regarded by the majority as imposed on franchises. Three of the Justices dissented because they thought the taxes were on property and not on franchises. One Massachusetts tax was on "the excess of the market value of all the capital stock of each corporation over the value of its real estate and machinery."[18] Mr. Justice Clifford for the majority gave weight to the fact that the Massachusetts court had held that the tax, if on property, would be invalid under the state constitution, but if on "commodities," signifying "convenience, privilege, profit, and gains," would not conflict with the state constitution. This seems hardly a satisfactory reason for withholding an independent Supreme Court analysis, unless state nomenclature is to determine national constitutional law. A second Massachusetts tax, entitled "An act to levy taxes ... on depositors in savings banks," provided that every institution for savings should pay "a tax on account of its depositors of three fourths of one percent per annum on the amount of its deposits."[19] {95} This foreshadows a distinction between corporation and stockholder recognized by the law in many ways. The third case denied to a Connecticut bank any deduction for United States bonds from an assessment under a statute requiring savings banks to pay "a sum equal to" a certain percentage of their deposits.[20] This language is so close to that of the New York statute, under which the Supreme Court pared down the assessment in the *Bank Tax* case[21] three years earlier, that one suspects some change of heart on the part of the Supreme Court majority.

Too numerous are the instances in constitutional law in which judicial lip service is rendered to a doctrine or a formula or a distinction although the dissenting opinions complain that there has been a departure from the previous application—too numerous to be enumerated. Sometimes the difference of judgment is confined to the characteristics of the situation involved, and this may be an isolated or a particularistic oddity or variation. Sometimes the difference between the Justices may turn on whether, in the particular case, form or substance shall have dominion. These two criteria lock horns in many legal forests. Some judges as individuals lean toward form; others lean toward substance. Still others lean now one way and now the other, according to which, in the particular instance, will best support a judgment based on other factors, often not clearly delineated. From a practical standpoint, from the viewpoint of the particular litigant and his counsel, such teeterings and see-sawings are signs of an undulating course of the law. Whether the law that undulates is constitutional law depends upon how constitutional law is classified and defined. {96}

Not infrequently a transparent departure from prior application of supposed principles or doctrine is the forerunner either of the overruling of precedents, or possibly of the creation of distinctions so finely drawn that one may doubt the degree of reverence in which they are held even by the imaginative artist who creates them. Illustrations of this may find mention later in this and other lectures.

The distinction between a tax on property or on income and a tax on a privilege measured by property or income drawn in the sixties found confirmation in *Home Insurance Company v. New York*[22] in 1890. This was a tax measured by applying to capital stock a rate which varied with the percent of dividends declared. Justices Miller and Harlan thought the tax "in effect" one on the property. The majority thought otherwise, unless they chose to overlook the dissenting term "in effect," but Mr. Justice Field's opinion is a gem of seeming contradictions. "The validity of the tax," he says, "can in no way be dependent upon the mode which the State may deem fit to adopt in fixing the amount for any year which it will exact for the franchise."[23] Yet earlier he had said of the immunity of government securities: "Nor can this inhibition upon the States be evaded by any change in the mode or form of the taxation, provided the same result is effected—that is, an impediment is thereby interposed to the exercise of a power of the United States."[24] This of course leaves open the question whether power to use immune capital or income in the measure of an excise on a corporate franchise does have the same effect as power to tax directly such property or income.

There may be no difference in some particular applications {97} of such a statute to a particular taxpayer, but, as will be submitted later, in other possible applications, there may be material differences between the two powers, both qualitatively and quantitatively.

Mr. Justice Field does not invoke this substantial element of the distinction, however much it may have influenced him, consciously or unconsciously. His main basis for decision is the distinction between the subject taxed and the measure for determining the amount of the tax. Perhaps as dominant with him, though not so explicitly elucidated, is the notion of conditioned privilege. This is the contention that to the grant of a privilege the state may annex a condition that would be beyond its power to impose as a direct demand with no warrant other than the fiscal desire for revenue. Mr. Justice Field, for all his strong *laissez faire* leanings, had a firm conviction that an artificial legal body, needing the exercise of the procreative power of the state to become a legal person, is peculiarly subject to dictation by its creative legal parent and should not be coddled when looking a gift horse in the mouth.[25] Mr. Justice Holmes was long infected with the same mechanical idea that in logic this is irresistible.[26] In many instances this may be fair enough when the only interest at stake is that of the individual or corporate recipient of a privilege that might be withheld or withdrawn. Such a favored grantee may within moderation be subjected to demands regarded as prices rather than completely coercive exactions, but this implication of consent does not automatically justify prices that {98} burden other interests like the borrowing power of the United States or the freedom of interstate commerce.

Before proceeding to the later wobbling of the privilege and subject-measure canons, it will be well to introduce parenthetically some rulings on collateral issues. In 1842 the court held that a state tax on "all offices and posts of profit" may not be imposed on a federal revenue agent.[27] In 1871 the court abandoned Marshall's suggestion that the nation may tax where the states may not, placed the immunity doctrine on the basis of reciprocity, and so held that the federal income tax might not be applied to the salary of a state judicial officer.[28] The reciprocity principle was applied again in the famous *Pollock* case, putting income from state bonds beyond the reach of federal income tax.[29] When Congress enacted the corporate excise of 1909, it included all the corporate income in the measure of the tax. This was sustained in 1911 in *Flint v. Stone Tracy Co,*[30] with its assessment on all income, including that from state securities. Neither such income nor any other income from property was then subject to direct national taxation, unless the tax on private income was duly apportioned among the states according to population. From the standpoint of national taxation, the enjoyment of a state granted corporate charter is not a privilege. The case had to rest on the subject-measure dichotomy.

With this long background, *Northwestern Mut. L. Ins. Co. v. Wisconsin*[31] came as a shock in 1927. Here a unanimous {99} Court held that the interest received from United States bonds may not be included in the assessment of a state license tax on domestic insurance companies. The tax was measured by gross receipts and was in lieu of all other taxes. Mr. Justice McReynolds does not deny the ancient doctrine. He merely declines to apply it. He says that the fundamental question is whether "the assessment must be regarded as a tax upon property or one on privileges or franchise of the corporation."[32] This he answers by asserting baldly:

> Here the statute undertook to impose a charge of three percent upon every dollar of interest received by the company from United States bonds. So much, in any event, the state took from these very receipts. This amounts, we think, to an imposition upon the bonds themselves, and goes beyond the power of the state.[33]

Here was realism galore, but it was new law. The opinion sought to distinguish the *Stone Tracy* case[34] because there the measure was net income, but the taxes sustained in the sixties[35] and in the *Home Insurance* case,[36] were measured by capital or something corresponding roughly to capital. Mr. Justice McReynolds blunders when he says that the charge in the *Home Insurance* case was measured by dividends. The measure applied to capital stock. It was the rate that varied according to the dividends paid. In the *Stone Tracy* case, it is true, the measure was net income and not gross. But both net and gross returns from state and federal bonds are equally immune from direct assessment by the companion government. The commerce clause distinction {100} between gross and net[37] had not heretofore been transferred to the field of intergovernmental relations.

Two terms later came the famous case of *Macallen Co. v. Massachusetts,*[38] which excluded from the measure of a state corporate excise the net income from United States bonds. Mr. Justice Sutherland recites the familiar distinction of earlier cases, but says that "It is implicit in all that the thing taxed in form was in fact and reality the subject aimed at, and that any burden put upon the non-taxable subject by its use as a measure of value was fortuitous and incidental."[39] The appropriate comment on this is that it is not true. Mr. Justice Field in *Home Insurance Co. v. New York*[40] had said that "No constitutional objection lies in the way of a legislative body prescribing any mode of measurement to determine the amount it will charge for the privileges it bestows,"[41] and had added that "It may well seek in this way to increase its revenue to the extent to which it has been cut off by exemption of other property from taxation."[42] In its setting this must have meant that if the state cannot tax certain property or income, it may change the tax to one on a privilege measured by that very property and income. This is just what Massachusetts did, which moves Mr. Justice Sutherland to say that the court "should be acute to distinguish between an exaction which in substance and reality is what it pretends to be, and a scheme to lay a tax upon a non-taxable subject by a deceptive use of words."[43] Elsewhere he speaks of an "artful use of words"[44] {101} and of "the adoption of a delusive name to characterize the tax or form of words to describe it. . . ."[45]

Naughty Massachusetts, there she stands, convicted because upon the recommendation of a commission[46] she changed her statute from one "on" income to one on the exercise of a privilege "measured" in part by income. She knew why she did it. It was to include the income from United States bonds in the measure and thus to get more than she could get by putting the tax "on" the income. Since Mr. Justice Sutherland thus sought to evade the established law without explicitly denying its validity in an appropriate setting, he exposed himself to correction and to a comment which will be quoted in a moment. In addition to charging intent to take advantage of a constitutional distinction, Mr. Justice Sutherland also seemed to regard this measure as one discriminating against income from federal securities, presumably because it treated that income as it treated other income. For this he cited *Miller v. Milwaukee*[47] which condemned a tax on dividends received by the stockholder with the exception of dividends which were the fruit of taxable corporate income. Thus the dividends taxed were those attributable to corporate income from United States bonds, and only those. This made the dividend tax discriminatory at one remove against interest on United States bonds. That was of course evil, if considered in isolation, but it was not the evil, if any, of the Massachusetts excise.

Before the next case in this particular subject-measure {102} series, Mr. Chief Justice Taft and Mr. Justice Sanford were succeeded by Mr. Chief Justice Hughes and Mr. Justice Roberts. This made a difference. In 1931 came *Educational Films Corp. v. Ward,*[48] in which the issue was whether income attributable to nationally granted copyrights may be included in the measure of a New York corporate excise. Instead of attacking the immunity of income flowing from patent rights and copyrights, which fell by the wayside the succeeding year, Mr. Justice Stone went straight to the subject-measure issue. He sustained the full measure of the excise on the authority of the *Home Insurance* and *Stone Tracy* cases.[49] This was easy if their authority had not been bedimmed. Mr. Justice Sutherland had refrained from overruling them in his *Macallen* opinion. Hence Mr. Justice Stone was able to escape from that case by pointing out that the New York measure was free from discrimination, and that New York had not amended its excise statute in order to include income from copyrights. So Mr. Justice Sutherland was hoist by his own petard in invoking the issues of intent and discrimination, which were easily handled. The distinction between the cases was thus pointed out by one of my colleagues when he was a student editor of the *Harvard Law Review.* This is how he put it:

> The recent decision in *Educational Films Corps. v. Ward* has apparently gone far to incorporate the law of torts into constitutional interpretation. An indirect intentional statutory invasion of the sanctity of governmental instrumentalities seems now void even without proof of resulting harm, while an indirect unintentional invasion is void only upon proof of damage to or undue burden upon such instrumentality.[50]

{103} Mr. Justice McReynolds joined without comment, but Justices Van Devanter, Sutherland and Butler dissented in the *Educational Films* case,[51] as had Justices Holmes, Brandeis, and Stone in the *Macallen* case.[52] The reasoning seems no longer important. Results are what count. It would be interesting to speculate why Mr. Justice Stone thought it wise to invoke the intellectual infelicities in Mr. Justice Sutherland's *Macallen* opinion to declare that that case did not stand in the way of the restoration of earlier law. These are arcana to which the outsiders are seldom admitted. I may perhaps observe, however, that once when I told my former Columbia colleague, after his elevation to higher state, that I noticed that he ducked a lot, he answered: "I know I do, and I hate it. But sometimes you have to do it to carry four colleagues with you." Another Justice, also a former colleague elsewhere, has indicated the same justification for what I had disapproved. So perhaps the new Chief Justice and his new brother needed a verbal bridge to cross back to the earlier shore. But the shore was clearly mapped when Mr. Justice Stone later said:

> Since the mere intent of the legislature to do that which the Constitution permits cannot deprive legislation of its constitutional validity, and the purposeful choice by the state of a method of taxation which appellee's contract allows, cannot alter the terms of the contract, the present act must be judged by its operation rather than by the motives which inspired it.[53]

The reference to contract had to do with another phase of the two cases.

It is not certain what the *Educational Films* case did to {104} the decisions on which the *Macallen* opinion had professed to rely. *Miller v. Milwaukee*[54] had condemned a dividend tax because the only dividends reached were those from corporate income that might not be directly taxed. But if no corporate income had been taxed, all dividends would have been taxable whatever their generation in the corporate portfolio.[55] Or if the corporate income had all been reached by use as a measure of assessment in an excise instead of being the subject of the imposition, then under earlier cases there would have been no constitutional immunity. In the use tax cases, discrimination is held to be avoided by considering the use tax and the sales tax together as parts of a single scheme.[56] The parallel may not be completely compelling because, in the *Miller v. Milwaukee* situation, the suggested alternative statutory devices would very likely not have identical results, owing to possible issues of jurisdiction over stockholders, to variation in deductions because of exemptions and expenses, and to top brackets for progressive rates—vagaries and varieties that might not be ironed out by Marshall's clear and simple theory of sovereignty.

A somewhat similar issue of discrimination had been decided against the Government in *National Life Insurance Co. v. United States*[57] in 1928. The insurance companies had gone to Congress with the consideration that their income from premiums, though taxable income, was not under state laws theirs to dispose of as they willed. They had to {105} pile up reserves to meet policy liabilities as they accrued. So they asked for an exemption. Congress granted an exemption of 4 percent of their reserves, assumed to be the income thereon, subject to the condition that this exemption should be curtailed to the extent of the ratio that any company enjoyed an immunity from taxation of income from state and federal securities. To this there was general agreement on the part of the companies. One company, however, objected and wanted the full exemption without diminution because of enjoying a constitutional immunity. Other companies regretted this departure from what they regarded as a gentleman's agreement between them and the Government, and hired Mr. Charles E. Hughes, then at large for such assignments, to argue in favor of the statutory plan. Notwithstanding his eminence and his excellence, he did not prevail. So National Life enjoyed its constitutional immunity with no string attached. There was a dissenting opinion by Mr. Justice Brandeis, concurred in by Justices Holmes and Stone.

The decision has always been a puzzling one to me, but, notwithstanding the line-up of the Justices, I am inclined to favor it. The issue is not one of logic or mathematics or accounting, but one of policy. The constitutionally exempt income was not taxed. By definition it could not be. But the free enjoyment of it was the determinant of the restriction of a favor. Why did the constitutional immunity obtain? Not primarily for the benefit of the taxpayer, but for the benefit of the borrowing government which undoubtedly borrowed more favorably because of the immunity of the interest paid. In saying this, one must recognize that with progressive income tax rates, those in the higher brackets {106} profit from the immunity more than the borrowing government gains thereby by reduction in the rate of interest it has to pay. It is an evil that the correspondence between the two is so imperfect. This might well merit remedy, if one could be worked out for each individual taxpayer. So far as I know, no such formula to secure correspondence has been devised. It is a rough-and-ready remedy to curtail the practical enjoyment of the constitutional immunity by using it to diminish a favor accorded on grounds of policy other than those that underlie the immunity. The policy behind granting the favor now under consideration is that the interest on the reserves must be stored up and added to them to meet capital obligations. Whether this justifies the favor is a matter that seems to me irrelevant. If the favor should be modified, should the extent of modification be determined by the enjoyment of a constitutional right?

It may of course be contended that since Congress may sanction taxation of its own securities by itself, as it now does,[58] it does not matter that, by some other device, it reduces the advantage to the nation of the prior immunity. But what of the immunity of income from state bonds? May Congress restrict the advantage of that immunity to a taxpayer who is *pro tanto* denied a favor because and only because of immune income from state securities? May Congress restrict the advantage accruing to a state from its lenders' obtaining the full fruit of constitutional immunity for interest on the state's securities? And with respect to the investors who have paid the public borrowers more because the interest is immune from taxation, are they not in effect being unfairly treated, if not cheated, when this {107} constitutional immunity is made a lever to deprive them of an advantage enjoyed by those who have not been lenders to government? Mr. Justice Brandeis in his dissent[59] seems rather insensitive to all this. He suggests other ways in which the value of the immunity may be reduced—by lower federal rates on income, by reduction in state taxation, by denial of any grace in inheritance taxation. He invokes *Flint v. Stone Tracy Co.*[60] for an erroneous assertion that this income from public bonds is taxable. He must have had in mind that it need not be considered immune as part of the measure of an excise tax on doing business in corporate form.

This latter point is a poser. It has long seemed strange to me that officials in Washington eager to repeal the immunity of state bonds altogether should not have continued the Corporate Excise of 1909 even after the

Sixteenth Amendment robbed the *Pollock* case of its primary power. From 1916 to 1926 the United States imposed a minuscule excise at one dollar or less per thousand dollars of capital stock, which was figured at full value with no deductions for immune securities.[61] There were contests over assessment, but no one went to the Supreme Court with claims of immunity. Evidently the bar assumed that it would be useless to quarrel about it. For the latter part of the period the {108} tax was imposed on trusts that behave like corporations though they have no charter from the state.[62] The justification had to be the invocation of the proper subject canon and not the privilege one. One wonders what the Court would say today if the activity selected as the subject were the clipping of coupons.

Even though the *Educational Films*[63] reassertion of *Flint v. Stone Tracy*[64] has remained steadfast ever since, it does not follow that the *National Life* device of curtailing favors to the extent of the receipt of constitutionally immune income or the ownership of immune capital would not still be disapproved. In a less drastic form it was condemned in the *Gehner* case[65] in 1930, Mr. Chief Justice Hughes concurring because of the *National Life* decision. Here a state in taxing the net assets of insurance companies in excess of real estate, allowed the deduction of reserves and unpaid policy claims only to the extent that the taxable assets bore to the total assets. This was shortly before *Educational Films*. So far as I am aware, the precise point has not arisen since. Readily distinguishable is *Denman v. Slayton*,[66] also in 1931, which held that the federal income tax may refuse to allow deduction of interest paid on indebtedness incurred to purchase or carry exempt municipal bonds. And in 1934 the Supreme Court declined to review a Court of Claims ruling that the carry-over of net loss to a succeeding year may be confined to the actual loss after inclusion of income from exempt securities.[67] {109}

For some reason Mr. Justice Stone preferred for some time to distinguish the *Macallen* case[68] instead of saying what was obvious about it. In 1933 in a memorandum opinion[69] the Supreme Court sustained a New York statute with an historical background similar to, if not identical with, that condemned in the *Macallen* case. So the absurd "intent" basis of that case evaporated, and the aroma of "discrimination" was never legitimately wafted upon it. The issues of discrimination have arisen frequently in connection with the application of the federal statute allowing a choice between various forms of state taxation of national banks and the stockholders' interests therein, subject to restrictions against burdens more serious than those imposed on "other moneyed capital."[70] Such problems resemble the ones involved in cutting down favors by reason of the enjoyment of constitutional immunities, but the two are not identical. Different also is *Helvering v. Independent Life Ins. Co.*,[71] which sustained a qualification on the deduction of expenses for servicing a building owned by an insurance company with occupancy shared by it and by tenants. The company was not allowed the maintenance deductions unless it included as a return the rental value of its own occupancy. An explicit tax on the rental value was declared to be a direct tax, requiring apportionment among the states, but it was held that this rental value was not taxed by being made a factor in determining the amount of deduction for expenses.

To return to the central issue of the distinction between {110} subject and measure. What can be the justification for permitting income and assets to determine the amount of a tax when they cannot be named as the subject of a tax? Is the difference like the puny one between Tweedledum and Tweedledee? In various instances of individual application it may well be this and nothing more. The rose smelled no sweeter for the Macallen Company by being called another name. The fragrance may have seemed sweeter to the Supreme Court in the *Educational Films* case,[72] but not to the taxpayer. The ruling distinction between the two cases is the intervening change in the composition of the Court. There should, however, be some justification for the restoration of the former law other than this. And there is, though it is a somewhat strange one. The justification is that from a realistic economic standpoint it is inconsistent to use as a measure what would be an improper subject. This is not the only spot in the law where inconsistency is wiser than harmony.

If the reciprocal immunities of state and national securities were an unmixed blessing in preventing burdens on borrowing governments, the blessing should not be evaded by any form of words. If the immunities create evil as well as good, there may be a place for the judgment of Solomon to divide the baby. There is no doubt that they do create evil as well as good. With high progressive rates of income taxation, the fortunate recipients in the high brackets profit more from the immunity of interest than do their less opulent neighbors. If the wealthy could absorb all the securities that governments cared to issue, the interest rate offered might reflect the value of the immunity to the purchasing {111} taxpayer with some fair degree of correspondence. This, however, is seldom if ever the case. Moreover, there are at least two taxing governments and many more borrow-ing governments. A state may be able to borrow cheaper money for roads and schoolhouses, but still lose disproportionately because of the tax-free haven for lenders to the United States. The gains and the losses all around simply do not "sugar off," as we say in Vermont.

Thus in addition to safeguarding against a burden on a borrowing government by the diminution in the taxing power of its counterpart in the federal system, the immunity confers a bounty on the public borrower, so long as competing private issues are subject to fiscal demands. This may be demonstrated more simply if we invoke the situation when public salaries enjoyed immunity. A state university and a private university could compete with each other on equal financial terms if there were no income taxes on the salaries of teachers. A ten-thousand-dollar salary from each institution would leave preference between them based on other considerations. The same equality between the two would prevail if the salaries paid by each were equally subject to income taxation. If, however, the salary from the private college were taxed, say at 10 percent, and the salary from the state university were constitutionally immune as it used to be,[73] then the state university is not only spared a burden but is presented with a bounty. Its nine-thousand-dollar salary is as good as its private sister's ten-thousand-dollar salary.

This suggests a possible situation in which the immunity {112} would enure fully to the benefit of the employing state. At the same time we do not know what the state loses because its citizens invest heavily in federal securities. The problems are more complicated and more variegated with different varieties of tax impositions affecting interest on public securities, with varying exemptions, deductions, rates and portfolios and salaries—what Mr. Justice Holmes might call a farrago of irrational irregularities[74] throughout. Hence, as a partial corrective, we may welcome the economic inconsistency of letting the left hand gather what the right hand must leave alone. The left-hand grasp upon the measure by which an excise on some privilege or proper subject is assessed may counterbalance the palsy of the right hand's failure, so that the two rules may be better than either one alone would be. Not only will the left hand not reach all the interest paid by the borrowing government, but what it reaches it will reach without danger of discrimination against it.

Where the measure is capital stock or income of a corporation, the assessment will be the same whatever the composition of the portfolio of the corporate taxpayer. There is no tax-free refuge in which the corporation may elude the collector. With a tax directly on capital or income, the investor may profit by hunting around and finding some sources of income that are free from a tax burden or may seem free even when not. He may think that he escapes fiscal burdens on stock in private corporations even though what the corporation itself pays may come out of him in the long run. No such escape or self-deception is open to the {113} corporate payer of tax demands measured by capital or income. Such demands, moreover, may be on a net worth or net income basis with various deductions and exemptions which keep the amount from rising dollar for dollar as the exempt capital or income ascends. Though the net income received by government from lessees of Indian or school lands is presumably still constitutionally tax exempt,[75] there remains a material difference whether the measurement of excises is on total assets without deduction for liabilities or on gross income without deduction for expense.

Business taxation differs in various respects from taxation of private investors who enjoy only unearned income. There is so little expense in storing certificates and clipping coupons that there is not likely to be great difference between gross income and net. Where, however, the subject of an exaction is business activity and not mere passive reaping where one has sown or not sown, there may be a large gap between gross and net returns. Where this is recognized in the admeasurement of excises, there is a difference of substance and not merely of form between subject and measure. Whether this has tacitly influenced the Justices who have apparently killed the *Macallen* case for keeps, we do not know, but it may be a factor of at least partial justification for its interment. Though net income from immune securities, unlike net income from interstate commerce, is still immune, the approval of its inclusion in a measure may still have grounds for grace other than the fact that it is economically inconsistent with the condemnation of a direct hit. {114}

The Constitution did not dictate that the states may tax net income from interstate commerce, but not net income from United States bonds. The Supreme Court dictated it. There is another contrast between the law on interstate commerce and the law on intergovernmental immunities. Both as commerce and as due process law *Western Union Telegraph Co. v. Kansas*[76] held in 1910 that a state may not measure an excise on doing local business by the total capital stock of the taxpayer, representing property scattered throughout the country. As due process law, *Trick v. Pennsylvania*[77] held in 1925 that a state of domicile may not measure an inheritance tax by chattels permanently located outside the state. These cases seem to me consistent, not in theory but in results, with the *Educational Films* case. The assessment of extraterritorial values is a sin of greater potentialities than is the inclusion of constitutionally immune income in the measure of a corporate excise. There is variation here, but not, in my judgment, vagary. The Constitution did well to suggest, however faintly, the distinction.

Allied to the distinction between subject and measure, but differing somewhat from it, is the distinction between the property of a corporation and the property of the stockholder. The point was first involved in *Van Allen v. Assessors*,[78] which held that the state may tax shares of stock in a national bank although the capital of the bank is all invested in stocks and bonds of the United States. This, however, was premised on the act of Congress permitting taxation of the shares. Three Justices dissented, thinking that the federal statute went no further than to deny immunity {115} of the shares because of the relation between the national bank and national functions, leaving untouched the issue as to the bank's investments. In *Cleveland Trust Co. v. Lander*,[79] however, the decision was followed in the case of a stockholder's interest in a bank chartered by the state, with respect to which Congress had, of course, been silent. In 1907 in a full dress opinion in *Home Savings Bank v. Des Moines,*[80] Mr. Justice Moody said that "the distinction between a tax upon shareholders and one on the corporate property, although established over dissent, has come to be inextricably mingled with all taxing systems, and cannot be disregarded without bringing them into confusion, which would be little short of chaos."[81] He seemed to disrelish the result, but said that the question is "one of power and not of economics."[82] The case is the more interesting because the Court had a hard time finding out whether the tax was on the bank or on the stockholder. The bank may be made to collect a tax that is regarded as one on the stockholder.

This insulation of the property of the stockholder in his stock and the property of the corporation in its assets has a long legal history behind it, though the veil may be pierced when it is deemed advisable. The result of the adjudicated separateness here has the same justification as the distinction between subject and measure and is perhaps more dictated by the practicalities. It must often be difficult to determine just how much of the value of the stock or of the dividends comes in any given year from the changing investments and returns of the corporation. I do not recall ever having come upon a contention that stockholders of a railroad may {116} secure commerce clause immunity, because some of the fruits of the railroad's activities are not open to direct state levies. The parallel is not perfect because the tangible property of the railroad has no immunity if the requisites of jurisdiction are satisfied. So far as I recall, I have never seen raised the issue whether a state may impose on a corporation an excise measured by all its capital or all its income, from whatever source derived, and in addition tax the shareholder's stock at its full value.

The phrase "from whatever source derived" at once invites consideration of the Sixteenth Amendment. In an involved literary peregrination, Mr. Chief Justice White said that this amendment added no new subjects to the national taxing power but merely removed from national taxation of income the requirement of apportionment among the states according to population.[83] There are contentions to the contrary for which I have little respect. I have read them and am persuaded that such a contention as that the design was to authorize Congress to tax any income that it chose is not sufficiently supported with clarity and widespread agreement or acquiescence as to justify the results that would flow from accepting it. For it would deprive the states of constitutional immunity and leave that of the nation unaffected. With all the evils in the criss-cross immunities, a partial offset is reciprocity between the states and the nation. The states should gain from the immunity of their securities from the national taxation what they lose by the immunity of national securities from their grasp. Nevertheless, it was blundering draftsmanship that left interpretation open to controversy. {117}

From the standpoint of state power, the taxation of inheritances is embraced within the privilege conception. So in 1896, *United States v. Perkins*[84] held that a state may tax a bequest to the United States. The tax was said not to be on the property but on its transmission. It is "in reality a limitation upon the power of a testator to bequeath his property to whom he pleases; a declaration that, in the exercise of that power, he shall contribute a certain percentage to the public use."[85] This of course derives from ancient conceptions of feudalism, hardly appropriate to the present era. On the basis of economics, this curtailment of a bequest to the United States is the clearest possible imposition of a burden, unless you choose to say that it is only a denial of a benefit, since the axe falls at a preliminary stage when there is only an incipient possibility of a windfall—a position I do not choose to endorse because it seems to me to assume the existence of a power which is the matter at issue—another instance of getting out of a major premise all that you put into it.

This seems to me quite different from allowing a state inheritance tax to be measured by all intangible investments, including United States bonds, sustained four years later in *Plummer v. Coler*.[86] I doubt if the market for government issues is greatly prejudiced by their inclusion with all comparable investments in the assessment of inheritance taxes, although it is clear that their immunity from being treated as competing private issues are treated confers upon them a distinct bounty. The comparison should be made between the absence of any inheritance tax on the one hand and the imposition of an all-inclusive one on the other hand, {118} and between the latter and one from which government issues are excluded by judicial fiat. The inheritance tax differs decidedly from a corporate excise measured by all capital or income, for the excise tax comes every year and the inheritance tax is occasional and spasmodic. I prefer this ground of decision to the privilege notion of arbitrary power.

The privilege notion lay behind the decision in *United States v. Fox*[87] in 1877, allowing a state to forbid a devise of land to the United States. But it had to be on a proper subject theory that Congress in *Knowlton v. Moore*[88] in 1900 was allowed to include state bonds in the assessment of the federal estate tax and that *Snyder v. Bettman*[89] in 1903 sanctioned a federal tax on a legacy to an Ohio city. The latter decision was not unanimous. When the judges differ, does the Constitution or some still higher law do the deciding? In so far as the federal tax on a legacy to a city exemplifies the principle of reciprocity between states and nation, there is not a little to be said for it, although it is more questionable than the inclusion of public securities in the assessment of state and national inheritance taxes. There is a lack of reciprocity in allowing a state to forbid a devise to the United States, because the United States has no corresponding regulatory power. It may well be, however, that the Court would allow Congress to forbid a trespass by the state on a national interest, even though the Constitution is not interpreted to do so. There are precedents[90] to invoke in favor of such sanction. {119}

During the brief regency when the *Macallen* case[91] was *locum tenens*, there was speculation whether its votaries would commit legicide of the rulings that inheritance taxes are not shackled by the intergovernmental relations principle. But on January 5, 1931, after the two new appointments, Mr. Chief Justice Hughes for a unanimous court said that profit from the sale of state and municipal bonds is taxable, and he cited the inheritance cases in support.[92] This was a week before *Educational Films*[93] smothered *Macallen*. The decision next to die was *Long v. Rockwood*,[94] which in 1928, over the dissents of Justices Holmes, Brandeis, Sutherland, and Stone, had held that a state may not tax royalties from patent rights conferred by the United States. This was explicitly and unanimously overruled in *Fox Film Corp. v. Doyal*[95] in 1932, which sustained a state excise on royalties from copyrights. Mr. Chief Justice Hughes said that "as the tax is measured by gross receipts," the *Educational Films* case is not applicable, and he put the case on the ground that copyright grants are not federal instrumentalities. This puts them in the same class as state charters of private corporations. The decision in *Gillespie v. Oklahoma*[96] in 1922 survived, though in waning health for sixteen years, in spite of its absurdity. This held that the lessees of oil and gas lands belonging to Indians and under restrictions by the United States may not be subjected to a state tax on income derived from operations under the lease. The absurdity lies in the fact that this is a second immunity in addition to the one on the rentals or royalties paid for the benefit of the Indians. Mr. Justice Holmes calls the tax {120} "a direct hamper upon the effort of the United States to make the best terms that it can for its wards."[97] Why not go still further and accord immunity to the wages of employees of the lessees, and from sales taxes on vendors to the lessees and so forth? Every additional immunity would aid in bargaining for higher royalties for the welfare of the Indians. The decision was doubtless influenced by an earlier case holding that the lessees may not be taxed on gross sales of coal from mines on Indian lands,[98] and perhaps by the fact that various states have been acute to profit all they can from Lo, the poor Indian.

How technical the Court could be in dealing with these taxes on government lessees was evident in 1931 and 1932 when in the *Group No. 1* case[99] income derived from sale of oil by a lessee of state land was held taxable by the United States where under the law of the state the lease is assumed to be a sale of the oil and gas, but immune in the *Coronado Oil* case[100] in which the lease was just a lease with right of extraction. Here four Justices dissented,[101] insisting that *Gillespie v. Oklahoma* should be overruled. And so it went in varying ways, varying with the kind of tax, varying with interpretations of state law, varying with different Justices, until in 1938 *Helvering v. Mountain Producers Corporation*,[102] with Justices McReynolds and Butler dissenting, denied immunity from the federal income tax for net income received as a result of operations by a lessee of state school lands. Mr. Chief Justice Hughes reviews the {121} earlier cases, finds that the distinctions between them have "attenuated" the "teaching" of the foundation case, and holds that the effect upon the Government of the tax on the lessees is not other than "remote" and "indirect." It would have saved the time of many of us and reduced the strain if a majority of the Court had appreciated this in 1922 when *Gillespie v. Oklahoma*[103] began the doctrinal wayward way.

A phase of this judicial cancellation of the judicial favor previously bestowed on government and on lessees of government by this gift of an immunity on top of an immunity deserves mention. Undoubtedly the lessees would pay higher royalties because their income was immune. Had Congress or a state by legislation conferred such an exemption, it could not be withdrawn. A state withdrawal would violate the obligation of contracts clause,[104] and a national withdrawal would violate the due process clause of the Fifth Amendment. This latter protection had been affirmed in condemning the repeal of a tax exemption previously contractually conferred on Indians or their lands[105] and in condemning an unfavorable change in a veterans' pension or insurance plan.[106] In the *Macallen* case, Mr. Justice Sutherland had without discussion declared flatly that the inclusion in the Massachusetts assessment of income from Massachusetts county and municipal bonds was void as impairing "the obligation of the statutory contract of the state by which such bonds were made exempt from state taxation."[107] It has since been held that a contractual exemption of capital is not impaired by taxation of the interest thereon by a general state tax on net {122} income,[108] but this is not relevant to our point about judicial cancellation of a judicially conferred immunity of lessee's income. It still remains something that could not be done by legislation which by binding contract first giveth and then later taketh away. Yet apparently it may be done by judicial giving and later taking, without blinking an eye. The same issue of the frustration of warranted expectations may arise by judicial withdrawal of judicially conferred favors to vendors and contractors. Blessed be the name of the Supreme Court.

Unjustifiable as was the immunity judicially conferred on lessees, a somewhat different attitude seems an appropriate one to take toward the story of sales and gross receipts taxes on vendors and contractors to the governments. A former trustee of Oberlin College informs me that Ohio's gross receipts tax as applied to a contractor made the college pay an added $30,000 for the construction of a dormitory. The estimated tax went into the bid along with the cost of labor and supplies. From an economic standpoint it makes no difference whether the tax is imposed on the seller or on the buyer, on the builder or on his patron, provided it is known in advance that the demand is certain. So in 1928, *Panhandle Oil Co. v. Mississippi*[109] acted with realism in holding that a state excise tax on vendors of gasoline measured by the number of gallons sold may not include gallons sold to the United States for the use of the Coast Guard fleet and a Veterans' Hospital. Similarly in 1931, *Indian Motorcycle Co. v. United States*[110] held that a federal excise on the sale of motorcycles may not be imposed on a sale by the manufacturer {123} to a municipal corporation for use of the police force. The United States contended that the tax was on combined manufacture and sale, but the majority regarded it as one on sale alone. Had the tax been on manufacture alone, it would not matter that the sale was to a public authority[111] or was one for export.[112] In either case, no deduction is necessary.

As manufacture is antecedent to sale and is correspondingly at one remove from a later vendee, so a tax on transportation was held in 1930 not to come within a legislatively granted exemption as one for the service of the governmental consignee.[113] And three years later it was held that a state university may not escape from a customs duty on imported scientific instruments, because the demand is an exercise of the commerce power and not of the taxing power.[114] An untrained legal analyst might have mistakenly assumed that it is both. Even an economist might wonder why names should make such a difference. When salaries of public officers still could claim immunity, it was held unanimously in 1926 that the federal net income tax may be imposed on the net income of an engineer even when it is the compensation for his services to a state in connection with a state water supply system.[115] The difference between the immunity of an official salary and the taxability of the contractor's compensation is not one which reflects the effect of the taxes on the employing government, but rather one {124} which relates to the permanence and directness and exclusiveness of the relation between the worker and his employer, the difference between an appointee and a hired man. It is sometimes easier to perceive distinctions and differences than to evaluate them, but the Constitution seems to be capable of both, at least from time to time.

Thus before the post-1937 reconstitution of the Court came two cases with differences more in form than in substance. In 1934, *Trinity farm Construction Co. v. Grosjean*[116] unanimously sustained the application of a state excise tax on gasoline used in the construction of levees by a contractor with the United States. In 1936, however, *Graves v. Texas Co.*[117] condemned a state tax upon storers of gasoline accruing at the time of withdrawal from storage, to the extent that the withdrawal was for the purpose of sale to the United States for the use of the Army, the Tennessee Valley Authority and the Department of the Interior. Here Mr. Justice Stone did not sit, and there was dissent from Justices Brandeis and Cardozo on the ground that the tax was on the privilege of storage and not on the sale. Consumption by a contractor as in the *Trinityfarm* case of course differs from storage by a prospective vendor, though both contractor and vendor are serving a government enterprise. However, the construction of the levees in the *Trinityfarm* case was declared not to be a governmental instrumentality, meaning, I assume, something that the Government was not doing for the sake of government.

Thus, the distinction between governmental and proprietary long familiar in the law of municipal liability for tort, has its recognized rôle in intergovernmental immunities and {125} may play a part psychologically in individual judicial voting even when it is not explicitly mentioned. The subjection of state proprietary business to federal taxation was first affirmed in *South Carolina v. United States*[118] in 1905, in which the federal internal revenue excise was applied to a state owned and managed liquor selling enterprise. Mr. Justice Brewer expressed apprehension that immunity of state business of this type might encourage the state to expand its functions indefinitely and thus to deprive the United States of long established sources of revenue. Justices White, Peckham, and McKenna dissented. The principle was reaffirmed in 1934 in *Ohio v. Helvering*,[119] also involving a state liquor business. Similar considerations played their part in condoning federal taxation of the salaries of public trustees of a street railway system of which the state was the operating lessee,[120] and state taxation of private enterprises conducted under federal licenses, and state property taxation of land owned by a licensee of the Federal Power Commission.[121]

These decisions on proprietary functions did not necessarily promise further abrogations of previously enjoyed immunities, but with the October, 1937, term begins a genuine abandonment of prior applications. The withdrawal of the immunity of lessees of public lands in 1938 has already been noted.[122] In the previous year came *James v. Dravo Contracting Co.*[123] which, over the dissent of Justices {126} McReynolds, Sutherland, Butler, and Roberts, sustained the application of the West Virginia Gross Sales and Income Tax Law to gross receipts derived from the performance of a contract with the United States for the construction of locks and dams. There is a suggestion in the opinion of Mr. Chief Justice Hughes that a government contractor is not a federal instrumentality so far as concerns a tax on his gross receipts, but the decision does not seem to be in any way influenced by the character of the work done. Presumably it would have been the same had the work consisted of the construction of public buildings to be devoted exclusively to legislative, executive, or judicial purposes. The nature of the construction did not prevent the dissent.

The opinion of the Chief Justice for the Court is characterized by his customary categorical power with invocation of analogies and careful confinement to the type of tax involved. The tax, he says, is not laid upon the government, its property or officers. It is not laid upon an instrumentality of government, for an independent contractor is not such an instrumentality. It is not laid on the contract with the government. It is nondiscriminatory. The fact that tax is not laid upon the contract is evidently designed to distinguish the cited sales tax cases and the case on withdrawal from storage. Of these the Chief Justice says that "[they] have been distinguished and must be deemed to be limited to their particular facts."[124] For this he quotes from the *Wheeler Lumber* case[125] which sustained the federal transportation tax as applied to lumber that the shipper had engaged to sell to a county for bridges. He invokes *Alward v. Johnson*[126] in support of taxes on receipts from contracts for {127} carriage of mail which were not on the carriage itself. All this is good analogizing and distinguishing, but misses what a realist would regard as the crucial point.

This is the economic point that the tax on gross receipts of the contractor increases *pro tanto* the cost to the government. The opinion does not seek to meet this point except obliquely by saying that the fact that the tax increases the cost of the government is not controlling, since the property tax on the contractor, which has always been sustained, also increases the cost. This is rather weak. The property tax comes but once a year. The gross receipts tax hits every dollar received. The opinion rejects as inapplicable here the commerce-clause differentiation between gross and net, because the commerce carriers and traders enjoy the constitutional immunity in their own right, whereas here the immunity claimed is that of the government and not that of the contractor, and the government disclaims the immunity. So the government did disclaim as part of its broader desire to end more of the immunities as constitutional ones. It has been intimated by some federal officers that this venture was more in the hearts of the national taxing authorities and the Department of Justice than in those of the Army and Navy and other extensive purchasing agencies of the United States.

A word may be invited by the statement that the enterprisers in interstate commerce enjoy the gross receipts immunity in their own right. Immediately and perhaps technically, yes. They must do the claiming, but so do the contractors here. But in neither case is the immunity conferred, for the sake of the interstate railroad or the government contractor. It is conferred to promote the freedom of {128} interstate commerce from undue state clogging in the one case, and in the other to keep the contracting governments from putting their hands in each others' pockets and interfering perhaps in various ways with the free conduct of public affairs, each by the other. This may be especially serious in the case of state taxation which decreases the purchasing power of the nation's dollar, often in a checkerboard fashion. Cantonments are built to a large extent where the weather is favorable. The making of airplanes, guns, ammunition, clothing and other commodities needed by the United States is not spread evenly over the land, acre by acre, or state by state. Should the United States be affected by state tax laws in its choice of producers? Should favored states reap special benefits flowing from the incomes of people in all the states of the nation? Such questions seem worthy of a consideration not accorded to them by the statement that a government contractor claims an immunity not in his own right but in that of the government.

The fact that the tax here was on gross returns while that sustained on the contracting engineer in *Metcalf & Eddy v. Mitchell*[127] was on net income is dealt with in a somewhat backhanded way. The difference between the two measures, it is said, does not determine the character of the agency. If the engineer had been regarded as a government instrumentality, even his net income would not at that time have been taxable under *Gillespie v. Oklahoma*.[128] The conclusion thus dimly adumbrated is that once it is determined that a contractor is not a governmental instrumentality, no taxing holds are barred. Obviously, this does not follow. Discrimination because the receipts, net or gross, come from {129} the government would be barred. So, whether assessments of gross receipts should be barred would seem to be an independent question. *Gillespie v. Oklahoma* was to vanish as law a year later. In the *Fox Film* case,[129] decided in 1932, the Chief Justice had said that as the tax there on income from copyrights was measured by gross receipts, the *Educational Films*[130] case is not applicable. The purpose of this was doubtless to clear the way for a direct overruling of *Long v. Rockwood*[131] on immunity of income from patent rights, and not to escape the issue by relying on the subject-measure device of *Educational Films*. It left, however, a possibility that the subject-measure canon might be confined to measures of net income and not of gross. This now seems to be dissipated by allowing a tax directly on gross receipts if the enterprise is not a governmental instrumentality, if we may trust an assumption that even though the subject is a governmental instrumentality, the measure is not. Who knows?

For the dissent, Mr. Justice Roberts insists that there is no difference between a gross receipts tax and a sales tax. This the Chief Justice does not deny, nor does he affirm. He shoves the point to one side by saying:

> And in dealing with the question of the taxability of such contrac-
> tors upon the fruits of their work, we are not bound to consider or
> decide how far immunity from taxation is to be deemed essential to
> the protection of Government in relation to its purchases of com-
> modities or whether the doctrine announced in the cases of that
> character which we have cited deserves revision or restriction.[132]

This was clear warning that the issue of direct taxation on sales to government was to be left open, without any new {130} commitment in favor
of immunity. It was puzzling at the time to any one who was inclined to
give weight to economic considerations, but as we have seen, economics is
not the only factor given judicial consideration in these matters. Later we
learned at least an explanation of the caution here, now that the Court
partitions its positives and its negatives according to the legal incidence of
the tax, and not according to economic incidence. Again, this seems to
cleave more to form than to substance, but this is but an added instance of
the perennial contest between the two.

In dissenting Mr. Justice Roberts seems to stretch the appropriate
time span when he says that "The judgment seems to me to overrule, *sub
silentio*, a century of precedents, and to leave the application of the rule
uncertain and unpredictable."[133] In fact, the judicially decreed immunity
of vendors started with the *Panhandle* case[134] in 1928. Immunity of an
independent contractor furnishing expert service was denied in *Metcalf &
Eddy v. Mitchell*[135] in 1926. With the *Trinity farm* and *Graves* cases[136]
intervening in 1934 and 1936, the next succeeding contractor case is the
Dravo case then at bar. What Mr. Justice Roberts does is to assume that a
hundred-year-old concept of intergovernmental immunities contained
initially all that he would later put within it. This is a fashion of many
lawyers and perhaps of some thinkers. Mr. Justice Roberts may have in
mind Marshall's decision on government bonds in 1829.[137] He thinks that
"There can be no difference in reason, or in practical effect, between
taxation of government contracts to repay borrowed funds or written
promises to pay for {131} goods previously furnished and a contract to pay
for goods and services as furnished. . . ."[138] Mr. Chief Justice Hughes, on
the other hand says that "There is no ineluctable logic which makes the
doctrine of immunity with respect to government bonds applicable to the
earnings of an independent contractor. . . ."[139] This should have been
obvious to Mr. Justice Roberts. He should have had his calamitous appre-
hensions assuaged by the reference by the Chief Justice to the power of
Congress to decree immunities not found by the Court in the Constitution
itself. This of course would not be true of the states. One who has suffered
long may sympathize with the dissenting anticipation of uncertainty and
unpredictability. This, however, was no novelty in this segment of the law.

The new law of the *Dravo* case was its disregard of *Graves v. Texas*[140] which the year before condemned the withdrawal tax on gasoline later sold to the United States. The Chief Justice says that the *Graves* case along with the sales tax cases must be "limited to their particular facts."[141] From an intellectual standpoint, it would have been welcome to have received light on why the withdrawal tax measured by volume was more unpalatable than the contractor's tax measured by dollars. Had the absence of differentiation appeared in a student essay instead of in a judicial opinion, questions would have been asked by the instructor. Though the sales tax cases may present issues of legal incidence, the withdrawal tax should have been free from them. The Chief Justice recognizes that this is a "difficult field to apply the practical criterion"[142] referred to in {132} previous cases, and his treatment of the problem does not incline one to disagree with him. Even Marshall's solvent of sovereignty is not self-executing.

With the judicial withdrawal of the constitutional immunities of government lessees and government contractors in 1936 and 1937, there was naturally curiosity to know what further immunities would topple next. The national authorities were desirous of bringing official salaries within the grasp of the taxing power, at least so far as national power was concerned. They prepared a memorandum relying in part on the words "from whatever source derived" in the Sixteenth Amendment.[143] And toward the end of the October, 1937, term, they argued successfully in *Helvering v. Gerhardt*[144] that the federal income tax may be applied to the salaries of employees of the Port of New York Authority. Their brief said that it was unnecessary to reconsider the earlier cases holding the salaries of public officials immune, because here the Port Authority was not engaged in an essential governmental function, and because the Port Authority was not created by the states alone but existed by virtue of an Act of Congress exercising its power over interstate commerce. The State of New York was joined by some twenty-four other states in arguing against the tax. The decision was premised on the ground that the Authority was not engaged in an essential governmental function, with a faint suggestion that Congress has greater powers than do the states.

This decision came down in May, 1938. The previous {133} year, in January, 1937, *New York* ex rel. *Rogers v. Graves*[145] had held unanimously, Mr. Justice Stone not sitting, that the New York net income tax must exclude from its assessment the salary of the General Counsel of the Panama Rail Road Company. The only issues argued in the opinion were over the status of the Road as a governmental agency and whether the General Counsel was an officer or an independent contractor. In March, 1937, *Brush v. Commissioner*[146] denied application of the federal income tax to the salary of the chief engineer of a municipal water system. Here

Mr. Justice Roberts dissented on the ground that the services rendered were of a type commonly rendered in ordinary commercial life. Mr. Justice Brandeis joined him. Justices Stone and Cardozo voted with the majority on the basis of a Treasury regulation assumed by them to confer exemption. In the absence of any challenge to the validity of the regulation it was said by them that "no opinion is expressed as to need for revision of the doctrine of implied immunities declared in earlier decisions."[147] This was a significant warning that the conception of a constitutional immunity might be open to change. It is interesting to observe here that both the United States and the State of New York did not wish their respective taxing powers eroded.

Though Mr. Justice Stone rests his opinion in the *Gerhardt* case[148] on the ground that the Port Authority is not engaged in an essential governmental function, not a little of his opinion appears applicable to all public salaries. A tax on income is not the same as a tax on capital. Possibly the United States is not subject to the same restrictions as are {134} the states. Perhaps *M'Culloch v. Maryland*[149] went too far in not being confined to discriminatory taxes. The effect on the employing government of a tax on the salaries of its employees is speculative. The taxes on independent contractors are sustained notwithstanding resulting increase of costs to government. Taxes on employees or officers impose no threat to the continued existence of the states. The taxing power of the United States is endangered if continually expanding state functions involve immunity of all official salaries. The immunity conferred by *Collector v. Day*[150] "was narrowly limited to a state judicial officer engaged in the performance of a function which pertained to state governments at the time the Constitution was adopted, without which no state 'could long preserve its existence.'"[151] Mr. Justice Black concurs specially and would abolish the "governmental vs. proprietary" dichotomy because it is so difficult of application. This neglects the fact that the distinction that the Court seemed to be groping for seems to be not that of an essential governmental function but of a governmental activity that does not find its counterpart in private enterprise. This would confine the salary immunity to judges and legislators and some executives.

By this creep-mouse, crawl-mouse progression, leg over leg the dog went to Dover, Dover here being *Graves v. New York* ex rel. *O'Keefe*[152] which on March 27, 1939, withdrew constitutional immunity from all salaries of officers and employees of state and national governments without regard to the nature of the public employment in which they are engaged. Mr. Justice Stone's reasons here were foreshadowed {135} in his *Gerhardt* opinion. The taxpayer here was an employee of the Home Owners' Loan Corporation, a lending entity created by federal statute[153] and wholly owned by the federal government, but Mr. Justice Stone took the broad ground that all constitutional national functions are governmental in character. He says that "The theory, which once won a qualified approval, that a tax on income is legally or economically a tax on its source, is no longer tenable. . . ."[154] For this he cites some recent cases on intergovernmental immunities and *Hale v. State Board*[155] holding that a contractual exemption from taxes on state bonds may rightly be held by the state court not to render the income therefrom immune from inclusion in a general income tax. He does not mention *Pollock v. Farmers' Loan & Trust Co.*[156] which held that such a tax may not constitutionally be imposed on income from state bonds. Conceivably this might lead one to infer that the Sixteenth Amendment, which removed the requirement of apportionment among the states from a national tax on income, has ended as well the intergovernmental aspect of that case. But there is no sign yet that it does. Congress, moreover, has posted a possibly effective guard to protect the immunity of government bond income,[157] and can undoubtedly give greater protection should need arise.

Here endeth the important part of the intergovernmental immunities lesson, especially for my main purpose of revealing {136} "Some Vagaries and Varieties in Constitutional Interpretation." Some of the more recent cases, as the long line of decisions on state taxation of national banks and their stockholders, are the product of judicial interpretation of Congressional consents, and some of Congressional inhibitions. Such were the cases wherein the Court denied certiorari from a circuit court decision holding income from bonds of the Port of New York Authority and the Triborough Bridge within a conferred Congressional immunity.[158] Such also was the decision holding national bank stock owned by the Reconstruction Finance Corporation within a national prohibition,[159] and one on a similar basis saving a Federal Land Bank from a state sales tax of $8.02 on lumber purchased to repair buildings acquired by foreclosure.[160] Constitutional and statutory elements were commingled in a decision permitting a state inheritance tax to apply to a devolution of Indian funds but not to one of Indian lands.[161] Four of the Justices were opposed to both, and four favored both. Mr. Justice Douglas was the essential fifth wheel that made the difference between the two. Congress had declared the land exempt from property taxation but had been silent with respect to the funds. It had not spoken about inheritance taxation.

In holding that a federal tax on admissions could be applied {137} to tickets for a football game conducted by a state university which used the proceeds for educational purposes, the Court assumed without deciding that "the tax is imposed directly on the State activity and directly burdens that activity" but nevertheless sustained the tax because the enterprise is commercial in character whatever the use of the proceeds.[162] In dissenting Mr. Justice Butler said that "It is hard to understand how the collection by the State of fees for the privilege of attendance brings, even for the purpose of federal taxation, its work of education to the level of selling intoxicating liquor . . . operating a railway ... or conducting any other commercial activity."[163] But the majority held the test to be, not the purpose for which the money was used, but the nature of the activity from which it was derived. The matter becomes of some importance under current federal income tax laws if state educational institutions emulate private ones and by purchase and lease back prosper along with their business lessees.[164]

Outside the proprietary exception, a tax directly on the government is condemned, at least where it is a state tax on the federal government. *Mayo v. United States*[165] in 1943 saved the United States from an inspection fee on fertilizer distributed to farmers without immediate charge but subject to later deduction from grants for soil conservation. The inspection also was forbidden. This was in essence a vendor sales tax on the benevolent government as charitable vendor.

Pennsylvania has a queer but ancient plan of adding the {138} value of machinery on the land of a bailee to the assessment of the land as though it were part of the land itself. The Mesta Company was a bailee of machinery owned by the United States and rented to Mesta at a rental of a dollar a year, to be used in the manufacture of guns on a cost-plus contract. It objected to the assessment so far as enhanced by the machinery it did not own. The United States intervened. The majority held that the machinery belonging to the Government was being taxed and ordered the assessment proportionately reduced.[166] It did not base the decision on the ground of economic burden, which was of course present under the cost-plus arrangement. Mr. Justice Jackson did not even call the tax one "on" the Government. It was merely on government property. Government property is usually in the possession of some officer, an agent or a contractor. It is immune as such government property.[167]

Justices Roberts and Frankfurter dissented. The former was a Philadelphia lawyer. The latter is a sharp though occasionally imaginative analyzer. They insist that the decision restores the test of economic burden, which Mr. Justice Jackson denies. He in effect treats the tax as one *in rem,* dismissing the Government as "an abstraction," and incarnating the machines and endowing them with an immunity of their own because of their owner. If this looks to the "legal incidence" of the tax, it is on the material inanimate and not on the abstract Government.[168] To the dissenters, there is something of a miracle resembling that at Cana in Galilee. To aliens from Pennsylvania the Keystone {139} notion may seem mere form, whereas to long indoctrinated Pennsylvania practitioners it may strike home as an unquestioned legal reality, as many another concept or fiction among lawyers' intellectual tools may seem realities for the purpose of legal use. Others less indoctrinated may be skeptical about the miracle of turning the machinery of one owner into the land of another. They may fear that if they give legal credit to such a miracle they will open the door to other legal legerdemain calculated primarily to deceive. After wars, the United States have surplus property to dispose of. They may become lessors of plants to lessees who install their own machinery. Should some state in which such plants are located add the value of the government owned real estate to the value of the privately owned machinery and pronounce it all machinery, the difference between such a miracle and the one credited by Justices Roberts and Frankfurter would seem to lie mainly if not wholly in the time of the first performance.

These competing miraculous legalisms with animistic incarnation on the one side and credulous acceptance of sheer make-believe on the other leave me in such a state of suspended judgment that I would be inclined to welcome a little bit of common sense to tip the balance, meaning an infusion of an economic judgment of where the burden falls. I know that this has received a majority of judicial votes against it and I know that the Court has refused to differentiate a cost-plus contract from one with a set designated price. But in those cases there were not the evenly matched contending aridities and falsehoods that there are here. So seldom does any issue of taxation of government property arise, that such a tax as that here can be sustained without {140} shackling judicial hands in dealing with different types of taxes. The matter may be unimportant, because in the particular result realism won. Why worry about fanciful theorizing pro and contra? The only answer may be that teachers are professional theorizers and that practicing the art or the propensity may be useful or at least fun for them and their students.

One may sympathize with Mr. Justice Jackson in his search for reasons, because three years earlier in *Alabama v. King & Boozer*[169] and in *Curry v. United States*[170] the Court had sustained a sales tax and a use tax, although there was no doubt that the economic burden fell on the United States. The Alabama sales tax was clearly imposed on the purchaser, though the seller was required to collect and remit the amount of the tax. King & Boozer were vendors to a contractor engaged in constructing an army camp for the United States, It was the first purchase by the contractor that was taxed. There was no intermediate possession taken by the contractor. Mr. Chief Justice Stone declared that "The circumstance that the title to the lumber passed to the Government on delivery does not obligate it to the contractor's vendor under a cost-plus contract more than under a lump sum contract."[171] The use tax in the *Curry* case was imposed on the use of roofing purchased outside the state by a contractor for the Government on a cost-plus contract and used by him in constructing an army camp at the camp site. The state court had condemned the tax. The

Supreme Court reversed. The opinion did not consider whether the taxing statute was applicable to use on a government reservation, {141} presumably leaving that to the state court upon remand.

The opinion of Mr. Chief Justice Stone carefully gave no hint of what would be held if legal incidence of the tax were clearly on the Government. It would seem that the condemnation of the fertilizer inspection fee in *Mayo v. United States*[172] in 1943 would be followed, and the test from now on would be, not "who is hurt, but who is hit."[173] In both the sales tax and use tax cases, the United States got into the contest, argued for immunity, and was defeated. The opinion gave weight to the state court's view of the state statute, saying that "Who, in any particular transaction like the present, is a 'purchaser' within the meaning of the statute, is a question of state law on which only the Supreme Court of Alabama can speak with final authority."[174] This apparently was the attitude of Mr. Justice Frankfurter in dissenting from the immunity accorded to government property in possession of a bailee,[175] but not in another case in which he said that the Supreme Court is not bound by "the descriptive pigeonhole into which a state court puts a tax."[176] So in the case on machinery taxed as real estate, the majority opinion declared:

> "Where a federal right is concerned we are not bound by the characterization given to a state tax by state courts or legislatures, or relieved by it from the duty of considering the real nature of the tax and its effect upon the federal right asserted." *Carpenter v. Shaw,* 180 U.S. 363, 367-68.[177]

Here are seeming contradictions that need clarifying.

Notes

1 4 Wheat. 316 (1819).

2 *Id.* at 426.

3 *Ibid.*

4 *Id.* at 429-30.

5 12 Wheat. 419 (1827).

6 *Id.* at 439.

7 4 Wheat. at 436.

8 *Id.* at 435.

9 *Id.* at 435-36.

10 *Id.* at 436.

11 Until Collector v. Day, 11 Wall. 113 (1871).

12 8 Wall. 533.

13 2 Pet. 449.

14 Bank of Commerce v. New York City, 2 Bl. 620; Bank of the Commonwealth v. New York City, noted at 2 Bl. 635, reported in 17 L. Ed. 456.

15 Laws of New York (1863), c. 240.

16 Bank Tax Case, 2 Wall. 200 (1865).

17 2 Wall, at 209.

18 Sustained, without reduction for the amount of United States bonds held, in Hamilton Company v. Massachusetts, 6 Wall. 632 (1868).

19 Sustained, without deduction for the bank's investment in United States bonds, in Provident Institution v. Massachusetts, 6 Wall. 611 (1868).

20 Society for Savings v. Coite, 6 Wall. 594 (1868).

21 *Supra* n. 16.

22 134 U.S. 594.

23 *Id.* at 600.

24 *Id.* at 598.

25 *Cf.* Field, J. in Maine v. Grand Trunk Ry., 142 U.S. 217 (1891), and Horn Silver Mining Co. v. New York, 143 U.S. 305 (1892).

26 *See, e.g.,* Holmes, J., dissenting in Western Union Telegraph Co. v. Kansas, 216 U.S. 1, 52 (1910).

27 Dobbins v. Commissioners of Erie County, 16 Pet. 435.

28 Collector v. Day, 11 Wall. 113.

29 Pollock v. Farmers' Loan & Trust Co., 157 U.S. 429, *opinion on rehearing* 158 U.S. 601 (1895).

30 220 U.S. 107.

31 275 U.S. 136.

32 *Id.* at 140.

33 *Id.* at 141.

34 *Supra* n. 30.

35 *Supra* n. 18-20.

36 *Supra* n. 22.

37 See United States Glue Co. v. Town of Oak Creek, 247 U.S. 321 (1918).

38 270 U.S. 620 (1020)

39 *Id.* at 628.

40 134 U.S. 594 (1890).

41 *Id.* at 600.

42 *Ibid.*

43 279 U.S. at 629.

44 *Id. at 630.*

45 *Id.* at 631.

46 Mass. 1925 House Documents, No. 233, quoted, 279 U.S. at 632-33.

47 272 U.S. 713 (1927).

48 282 U.S. 379.

49 *Supra* n. 22, 30.

50 Note (1931), 44 HARV. L. REV. 829.

51 *Supra* n. 48.

52 *Supra* n. 38.

53 Pacific Co. v. Johnson, 285 U.S. 480, 495-96 (1932).

54 *Supra* n. 47.

55 272 U.S. at 714, citing Des Moines Natl. Bk. v. Fairweather, 263 U.S. 103 (1923).

56 Gregg Dyeing Co. v. Query, 286 U.S. 472 (1932); Henneford v. Silas Mason Co., 300 U.S. 577 (1937).

57 277 U.S. 508.

58 Public Debt Act of 1941; *cf.* INT. REV. CODE § 103 (1954).

59 277 U.S. 508, 522.

60 220 U.S. 107 (1911) .

61 Revenue Act of 1916, § 407; Revenue Act of 1918, § 1000; Revenue Act of 1921, § 1000; Revenue Act of 1924, § 700. The small capital stock tax imposed by § 215 of the National Industrial Recovery Act of 1933 and carried forward as §1200 of the Internal Revenue Code of 1939 until repealed by § 201 of the Revenue Act of 1945 was unlikely to produce contest since the tax was based upon a declared value freely chosen, and the taxpayer was interested in declaring a value adequately high to reduce to a minimum a related and more onerous excess profits tax.

62 Revenue Act of 1918, § 1; Revenue Act of 1921, § 2 (2); Revenue Act of 1924, § 2 (a) (2).

63 *Supra* n. 48.

64 *Supra* n. 60.

65 Missouri *ex rel.* Missouri Ins. Co. v. Gehner, 281 U.S. 313.

66 282 U.S. 514.

67 Phila. Fire & Marine Ins. Co. v. U.S., 3 F. Supp. 655 (1933), *cert. denied,* 290 U.S. 703.

68 *Supra* n. 38.

69 New York *ex rel.* Northern Finance Corp. v. Lynch, 290 U.S. 601.

70 REV. STAT., § 5219 (1875), 12 U.S.C. § 548 (1952).

71 292 U.S. 371 (1934).

72 *Supra* n. 48.

73 Under Collector v. Day, 11 Wall. 113 (1871). *Cf. e.g.,* I.T. 2677, XII, 1 CUM. BULL. 141 (1933).

74 See Gast Realty and Investment Co. v. Schneider Granite Co., 240 U.S. 55, 59 (1916).

75 See Murphy, J., dissenting in Oklahoma Tax Comm. v. U.S., 319 U.S. 598, 615 (1943). *Cf.* Powell, *State Inheritance Taxes on Indians* (1944), 44 COL. L. REV. 836.

76 216 U.S. 1.

77 268 U.S. 473 (1925).

78 3 Wall. 573 (1866).

79 184 U.S. 111 (1002).

80 205 U.S. 503.

81 *Id.* at 518.

82 *Id.* at 519.

83 Brushaber v. Union Pacific R.R., 240 U.S. 1 (1916).

84 163 U.S. 625.

85 *Id.* at 628.

86 178 U.S. 115 (1900).

87 94 U.S. 315.

88 178 U.S. 41.

89 190 U.S. 249.

90 *Cf.* Board of Commrs. v. Seber, 318 U.S. 705 (1943) with Shaw v. Gibson-Zahniser Oil Corp., 276 U.S. 575 (1928). See also Carson v. Roane-Anderson Co., 342 U.S. 232 (1952).

91 *Supra* n. 28.

92 Willcuts v. Bunn, 282 U.S. 216.

93 *Supra* n. 48.

94 277 U.S. 142.

95 286 U.S. 123.

96 257 U.S. 501.

97 *Id.* at 506.

98 Choctaw, Oklahoma & Gulf R.R. v. Harrison, 235 U.S. 292 (1914).

99 Group No. 1 Oil Corp. v. Bass, 283 U.S. 279.

100 Burnet v. Coronado Oil & Gas Co., 285 U.S. 393.

101 Justices Brandeis, Stone, Roberts, and Cardozo.

102 303 U.S. 376.

103 *Supra* n. 96.

104 New Jersey v. Wilson, 7 Cr. 164 (1812).

105 Choate v. Trapp, 224 U.S. 665 (1912).

106 Lynch v. United States, 292 U.S. 571 (1934).

107 279 U.S. 620, 634 (1929).

108 Hale v. State Board, 302 U.S. 95 (1937).

109 277 U.S. 218.

110 283 U.S. 570.

111 Liggett & Myers Tobacco Co. v. United States, 299 U.S. 383 (1937).

112 Cornell v. Coyne, 192 U.S. 418 (1904).

113 Wheeler Lumber Company v. United States, 281 U.S. 572.

114 Board of Trustees v. United States, 289 U.S. 48 (1933).

115 Metcalf & Eddy v. Mitchell, 269 U.S. 514.

116 291 U.S. 466.

117 298 U.S. 393.

118 199 U.S. 437.

119 292 U.S. 360.

120 Helvering v. Powers, 293 U.S. 214 (1934).

121 Federal Compress Co. v. McLean, 291 U.S. 17 (1934); Susquehanna Power Co. v. State Tax Comm., 283 U.S. 291 (1931).

122 Helvering v. Mountain Producers Corp., 303 U.S. 376 (1938).

123 302 U.S. 134.

124 *Id.* at 151.

125 *Supra* n. 113.

126 282 U.S. 509 (1931).

127 *Supra* n. 115.

128 *Supra* n. 96.

129 *Supra* n. 95.

130 *Supra* n. 48.

131 *Supra* n. 94.

132 302 U.S. at 153.

133 *Id.* at 161.

134 *Supra* n. 109.

135 *Supra* n. 115

136 *Supra* n. 116-17.

137 Weston v. Charleston, 2 Pet. 449.

138 302 U.S. at 168.

139 *Id.* at 152.

140 *Supra* n. 117.

141 302 U.S. at 151.

142 *Id.* at 152.

143 TAXATION OF GOVERNMENT BONDHOLDERS AND EMPLOYEES (Washington, 1938).

144 304 U.S. 405 (1938).

145 299 U.S. 401.

146 300 U.S. 352.

147 *Id.* at 374.

148 *Supra* n. 144.

149 *Supra* n. 1.

150 *Supra* n. 28.

151 304 U.S. at 415.

152 306 U.S. 466.

153 Home Owners' Loan Act of 1933, 48 STAT. 128.

154 306 U.S. at 480.

155 *Supra* n. 108.

156 *Supra* n. 29.

157 31 U.S.C. § 742. Doubt as to the effectiveness of this provision with respect to state income taxes may arise from comparison of its terms with those of the Iowa statutes considered in Hale v. State Board, 302 U.S. 95 (1937). *Cf.* Smith v. Davis, 323 U.S. 111 (1945).

158 Commr. v. Shamberg's Estate, 144 F.2d 998 (CA. 2, 1944), *cert. denied,* 323 U.S. 792 (1945); Commr. v. White's Estate, 144 F.2d 1019 (CA. 2, 1944), *cert, denied,* 323 U.S. 792 (1945).

159 Maricopa County v. Valley National Bank, 318 U.S. 357 (1943). *Cf.* Baltimore National Bank v. State Tax Comm., 297 U.S. 209 (1936).

160 Federal Land Bank v. Bismarck Lumber Company, 314 U.S. 95 (1941).

161 Oklahoma Tax Comm. v. United States, 319 U.S. 598 (1943). For more extended comment and analysis, see Powell, *State Inheritance Taxes on Indians,* 44 COL. L. REV. 836 (1944).

162 Allen v. Regents, 304 U.S. 439 (1938). *Cf.* New York v. United States, 326 U.S. 572 (1946).

163 304 U.S. at 457.

164 See INT. REV. CODE §§ 511-14 (1954), noting particularly § 511 (a) (2) (B).

165 319 U.S. 441.

166 United States v. Allegheny County, 322 U.S. 174 (1944).

167 Van Brocklin v. Tennessee, 117 U.S. 151 (1886).

168 322 U.S. at 181-89.

169 314 U.S. 1 (1941).

170 314 U.S. 14 (1941).

171 314 U.S. at 13-14.

172 *Supra* n. 165.

173 *Cf.* Kern-Limerick, Inc. v. Scurlock, 347 U.S. 110 (1954).

174 314 U.S. at 9-10.

175 322 U.S. at 197-98.

176 Wisconsin v. J.C. Penney Co., 311 U.S. 435, 443 (1940).

177 322 U.S. at 184.

V. Federalism: State Powers Affecting the National Economy; State Police Power

{142}

AGAIN, of necessity, we begin with Marshall. From the standpoint of actual decision, *Gibbons v. Ogden*[1] in 1824 told us what was obvious from the supremacy clause of the Constitution.[2] State laws in conflict with valid Congressional enactments are inoperative so long as the national legislation remains unchanged. The questionable part of Marshall's ruling is that the coasting license conferred under an act of Congress includes authority to sail by steam propulsion between points in two different states. Justice Johnson in the Supreme Court,[3] and Kent and other New York state judges thought otherwise,[4] and Marshall himself neglected the point a few years later.[5] Marshall's error, if error it was, was in the field of statutory interpretation, not in that of constitutional law. Congress might have changed its statute prospectively, had it so desired. It might have left its statute unchanged and passed an independent one, recognizing the existence of state power, as it did with control of pilots, intoxicating liquor, and prison-made goods, to which we shall advert later.

{143}

As soon as Marshall declared briefly that Congress was already regulating the navigation here, it was quite unnecessary for him to consider whether the states may regulate commerce in the absence of any relevant national action. He nevertheless proceeds to do so before giving his detailed analysis of the privilege that the coasting license confers. To the argument that the commerce power is indivisible and that therefore Congress has it all and the states have none, Marshall's comment is that there is great force in the argument and the Court is not satisfied that it has been refuted.[6] This is passing a qualified judgment on the merits of a debate, and not declaring a point of law. Since the point was no longer relevant, Marshall may perhaps be forgiven for not dealing with its substantively. He did declare that if there is collision between the national and the state legislation, it is immaterial whether the state law is passed "in virtue of a concurrent power 'to regulate commerce . . . ,' or, in virtue of a power to regulate their domestic trade and police."[7]

This subordination of state laws, however they may be characterized, keeps Marshall from immediate danger in recognizing that the Constitution clearly assumes that the states retain a power to apply inspection laws to imports and exports. He however cannot admit that a power to regulate commerce is the source of this inspection power. In so far as this means only that this power is not as broad as the commerce power of Congress, it must be undeniable even in the absence of any expressed constitutional restriction, for a legislative authority confined within the boundary lines of a single state cannot apply to the area of a nation as may the {144} power of Congress. If Marshall means more than this, he only indicates a possible and still broader pronouncement that the Federal Constitution is not the "source" of any state power except a few having to do with national elections and the process of constitutional amendment. State powers are derived from Great Britain, *vi et armis*. State legislatures have the legislative powers of Parliament, except so far as they have been denied or restricted by the state or the federal constitutions. Their powers do not in general even have to have a name, as do the national powers. The exceptions are not here relevant.

Marshall's gifts for debating and sermonizing might make some of his isolated statements seem more restrictive of state power than careful study of his whole opinion would warrant. In indicating what state police power may do with respect to commerce, he does not confine it to inspection laws. In speaking of the "immense mass of legislation" still belonging to the states he includes "Inspection laws, quarantine laws, health laws of every description" as well as laws "which respect turnpike roads, ferries, etc. . . ."[8] So it really did not matter greatly that he doubts whether the states have any power that may rightly be named a commerce power. And five years later, in *Willson v. Black Bird Creek Marsh Company*,[9] he sustained the power of Delaware to authorize the construction of a dam which barred ships from sailing up a small navigable tidal creek on voyages to and from salt water. Very briefly Marshall gives the practical justification for draining the marsh, enhancing the value of the property and perhaps improving the health of the inhabitants, and says, ". . . measures calculated to {145} produce these objects, provided they do not come into collision with the powers of the general government, are undoubtedly within those which are reserved to the states. . . He concludes that "We do not think" that the statute authorizing the dam, "can, under all the circumstances of the case, be considered as repugnant to the power to regulate commerce in its dormant state, or as being in conflict with any law passed on the subject."[10]

From the standpoint of the wording of the Tenth Amendment, Marshall might well have avoided using the phrase "reserved to the states," for the "reserved powers" are those not given to Congress nor prohibited to the states. Technically the "reserved powers of the states" are those that Congress may not negative or perhaps not encroach upon; but the matter is hardly so simple, because Congress by one power, such for example as the war power, may supersede state laws enacted under a different and still surviving state power. Of this, of course, Marshall was fully aware when he said that measures of the states and of the nation may so resemble each other as to be confusing, but added that this does not prove that the powers from which they proceed are identical.[11] Yet for this and perhaps other reasons, it seems to me precarious to use too loosely the word "reserved." Mr. Justice Swayne was certainly careless in *Gilman v. Philadelphia*[12] in 1866 when, on the authority of the *Black Bird Creek* case, he sustained state authorization of a bridge which would be not more than thirty feet above high water level and which would obstruct some navigation of the Schuylkill and said: {146}

> Until the dormant power of the Constitution is awakened and made effective, by appropriate legislation, the reserved power of the States is plenary, and its exercise in good faith cannot be made the subject of review by this court.[13]

"Reserved" and "plenary"—and this fourteen years after the Wheeling Bridge at the suit of Pennsylvania had been declared an invalid obstruction to commerce on the Ohio river.[14]

In the *Black Bird Creek Marsh* case Marshall does not advert to the stated fact that the vessel in question was licensed and enrolled for the coasting trade. In the *Gilman* case Mr. Justice Swayne notes that the point was brought up by counsel and that "The court was silent upon the subject," from which he concludes:

> A distinct denial of its materiality would not have been more significant. It seemed to have been deemed of too little consequence to require notice. Without overruling the authority of that adjudication, we cannot, by our judgment, annul the law of Pennsylvania.[15]

How convenient it would be for all of us if we could thus iron out difficulties and inconsistencies *sub silentio*. Mr. Justice Clifford, concurring in *Hall v. DeCuir*,[16] was more vocal in an effort at reconciliation. He says that Congress had not assumed to control state legislation over small navigable creeks into which the tide flows, since these are never classified as public navigable waters, though they are capable of being navigated by small vessels when the tide {147} is full. This is mere guesswork of statutory interpretation, which Marshall preferred not to venture upon.

Marshall participated in but one more argument on the power of the states to regulate interstate commerce. This was *Mayor of New York v. Miln,* which involved the constitutionality of a New York statute requiring masters of vessels to report the names of passengers from other states and from foreign countries, together with other information about them. The case was argued during the 1834 term, and later postponed for reargument, because, as Marshall announced, "four judges do not concur in opinion as to the constitutional questions which have been argued."[17] The cases were again continued in 1835.[18] On July 6 of that year, John Marshall died in Philadelphia. On December 28, 1835, President Jackson sent to the Senate the nomination of Roger Brooke Taney as Chief Justice and that of Philip P. Barbour as Associate Justice. Taney had earlier been nominated to fill the vacancy in the Associate Justiceship to which Barbour was now appointed, but the Senate had postponed indefinitely action on confirmation. He was finally confirmed for the higher post on March 15, 1836, by a vote of twenty-nine to fifteen. The *Miln* case was reargued and decided in the January term, 1837.[19]

Mr. Justice Story was the only dissenter in the case. He is undoubtedly on firm ground in saying that Marshall after the first argument had agreed that the state law was invalid. He is on less solid ground when he declares that Marshall had held that the commerce power of Congress is exclusive.[20] He puts as Marshall's own views some arguments {148} of counsel which he had called "of great force," adding only that the Court was not satisfied that they had been refuted. The opinion for the Court in the *Miln* case was by the new Associate Justice, Philip Barbour. It declares that it is not necessary to decide whether the commerce power of Congress is exclusive, because this requirement of filing reports on passengers after their landing is good as a police measure. Mr. Justice Thompson wrote a concurring opinion holding the statute valid both as a police measure and as a regulation of commerce in the absence of relevant regulation by Congress.

It is familiar learning that this issue of state power was enmeshed with theories of state sovereignty and of state power over commerce in slaves. The latter question came before the Court in *Groves v. Slaughter*[21] in 1841 in a suit on a note for the price of slaves brought into Mississippi for sale. The constitution of Mississippi prohibited such introduction for sale. The question was whether this rendered the note invalid. The Court passed by on the other side by ruling that, in the absence of any enforcing legislation by Mississippi, the question of the validity of the state constitutional ban was not properly open for consideration. Taney and McLean wrote separate opinions sanctioning state power to exclude. The other Justices were noncommittal. This disposition of the dispute might be thought by some to be in the nature of a dodge, but such unassertiveness is not entirely unknown in constitutional law even in its later days.

Six years later came cases involving the application of the liquor laws of three states, reported collectively under the {149} caption of the *License Cases*.[22] Taney wrote what seems to me a masterly opinion drawing at length from the opinion in *Brown v. Maryland*[23] a case about which he knew almost as much as Marshall knew about the commissions of those Justices of the Peace involved in *Marbury v. Madison*.[24] Taney in his *License* opinion avers that at the time he thought his contentions for the state in *Brown v. Maryland* were right, but that mature reflection had convinced him that the decision was wise. The main justification he gives is that imports from abroad will be landed mostly in the maritime states, though many will proceed to the interior. If the maritime states may tax the first sale in the original package, they may take toll from consumers throughout the nation. This was true enough in Taney's time. Now, however, the interior states may be importing states, as Ohio learned when it found itself forbidden to collect a property tax on hemp brought from abroad to Xenia, Ohio, and awaiting processing there while still unsold and in the original package.[25]

The liquor involved in the *License Cases* from Rhode Island and Massachusetts came from abroad, and its importation was authorized by Congress. The sales, however, were of portions withdrawn from the casks from across the sea. So very easily, taking advantage of the concessions his contentions in *Brown v. Maryland* had wrung from Marshall, Taney could rule that these sales were of articles no longer in foreign commerce, and hence were local and subject to state power. He conceded that state power at this stage may {150} to a degree discourage importation, but nevertheless this internal traffic is for the states to control. In the New Hampshire case, the indictment was for an unlicensed sale of a full barrel of gin brought in from Boston. Marshall had said that he supposed the principles of *Brown v. Maryland* to apply to importations from a sister state, but that was *obiter*, and the technical basis of the immunity decreed for the sale of goods from abroad was that Congress had regulated the importation, and the state law was in conflict with the permission implied in the national legislation. Hence Taney here could neatly hoist his predecessor by his own petard. Congress had not regulated interstate commerce. Hence *Brown v. Maryland* does not apply.

Hence the question of New Hampshire's power over this barrel of gin was an open one. With telling analysis Taney for himself insists that the power given to Congress by the commerce clause is not in and of itself an inhibition on all state power. He invokes long continued and uncontested practice by the states, he adduces recognition by Marshall and others that under a name other than a commerce power the states may deal with commerce, and he insists that these are regulations of commerce, as any plain and clear-sighted man would have to concede. Taney's mind seems to me markedly neater than that of Marshall, and his arguments are less open to refutation. Marshall was more intricate, more philosophical, cleverer at turning sharp corners, and his elocution is more sonorous than Taney's—gifts which doubtless are literary virtues but not necessarily judicial ones. Marshall was a nation builder, which Taney was not. As a creative statesman Marshall built superstructures on the foundation laid by the Fathers, but Taney in my view {151} kept closer to that foundation than did Marshall, with always the tragic exception of his *Dred Scott* enormity as to the absence of national power to forbid slavery in the territories.[26]

The nine Justices participating in the *License Cases* were unanimous, that is to say unanimous in everything but the reasons for the decision. Some of them agreed with Taney on the idea of a concurrent commerce power in the states. Others preferred to rest the result on the reserved police power of the states. There were interminably long opinions. There must have been ulterior reasons why they differed so fully in theory and not in results. For me it seems so simple to say that these laws derived from a police power which may apply though they regulate the commerce that Congress may regulate by its commerce power. Mr. Justice Catron gives us the reason why this is to be classified as police power rather than as taxing power. It was, he says, "admitted on the argument, that no licenses are issued, and that exclusion exists, so far as the laws can produce the result—at least, in some of the States,—and that this was the policy of the law."[27] The classification, as between police and taxing power, becomes important later because of the distinction drawn between the times at which they may impinge on products from sister states.

Presumably the laws condemned two years later in the *Passenger Cases*[28] should be classified as exercises of the power of taxation though there was effort in argument to regard them as police measures. They levied taxes on the master of every vessel landing passengers, with authorization {152} for him to recoup them from the entrants. The police justification sought to be adduced was that some of the funds were to be used for the relief of foreign paupers. The majority held, however, that the states may not put a tax upon the landing of passengers in interstate and foreign commerce, whatever the use of the proceeds. Taney, Daniel, Nelson, and Woodbury dissented. Taney insisted that it had become established that the states enjoy a concurrent power over commerce. If we might compare the decisions of this era in terms of their results without caring about the theory or what I might dub the lexogonamy, we might be better satisfied than we are when wading through the too voluminous and too numerous opinions. Their composition must have taken a long time if the authors had to write them out in long hand.

In 1851 a majority of the Court made substantial progress in dealing with the exclusive-concurrent imbroglio. This was in *Cooley v. Board of Port Wardens,*[29] which sustained a statute of Pennsylvania requiring masters of vessels to take on pilots or pay half pilotage fees to go to the use of the Society for the Relief of Distressed and Decayed Pilots. To the question whether the power of Congress is exclusive, Mr. Justice Curtis took a great step forward by answering: "Yes, and No." This is the wisest initial answer to give to many questions that embrace such a variety and diversity of issues that no single answer can possibly be suitable for all. So much footless debate between disputants might be avoided if broad barn-door questions were split up into subordinate and more particular problems, inviting separate and independent analysis and judgment. This is akin to the {153} false either-or dichotomy that judges are often prone to fool with—either commerce or police power, when it is both. Granted that it is but a first step to say "Yes and No," or "Sometimes Yes and sometimes No," such an answer leads to the next inquiry: When and why, Yes? When and why, No?

Mr. Justice Curtis says that the nature of the commerce power depends upon the nature of the subjects over which it is exercised and he continues:

> Now the power to regulate commerce, embraces a vast field, containing not only many, but exceedingly various subjects, quite unlike in their nature; some imperatively demanding a single uniform rule, operating equally on the commerce of the United States in every port; and some, like the subject now in question, as imperatively demanding that diversity, which alone can meet the local necessities of navigation.[30]

This is well enough for the easy cases at either end of the scale. But there are harder cases not covered by the formula. For some subjects do not imperatively demand either uniformity or diversity of regulatory rules. They will admit of either. So later judges have sometimes rephrased it to speak of subjects which "admit of" uniformity and subjects which "admit of" diversity. This covers all, without a gap. The trouble is, however, that the zones somewhat intersect, so that instead of subjects in neither class, some of the subjects are in both. Which is the undistributed middle, I must leave to others. Wise judges have occasionally stated only one side. Here you can make an inclusive classification, but what you include in each side depends upon how you begin the statement. If you say that the power is exclusive over {154} subjects that admit of uniformity but concurrent over those that do not, you favor the exclusive group. If you say that the power of the states is concurrent over those subjects that admit of diversity, you widen the scope of state power.

Mr. Justice Curtis did somewhat better when he came to consider the regulation of pilots in the case at bar. He speaks of an act of Congress in 1789 which left the subject to the states, as manifesting its understanding that the subject did not require its exclusive legislation and then says that "the nature of the subject when examined, is such as to leave no doubt of the superior fitness and propriety, not to say the absolute necessity, of different systems of regulation, drawn from local knowledge and experience, and conformed to local wants."[31] Of course this Janus phrase "not to say" means either to suggest it or not to suggest it. But "superior fitness and propriety" is quite adequate. It would not take care of the fifty-fifty cases if there were such an even balance in any subject, but it will do for a major premise if the judges will include in the minor premise of "superior fitness" any subject that they think should be regulated by the states and will exclude from it any that they would designate as one for Congress alone. Other shorthand captions for the two groups of subjects are uniformity versus diversity, and national versus local. The local subjects are subjects of interstate commerce where diversity of regulation is preferred.

In saying that the nature of the power is determined by the nature of the subject over which it is exercised, Mr. Justice Curtis fails to take into account the nature of the regulation. Here the regulation was a requirement to take on pilots or contribute to a fund. Suppose the regulation {155} were a prohibition against using a pilot, is it conceivable that any court would sustain it? The parade of decisions since the *Cooley* case makes it clear that the particular regulation involved is one of the factors in the problem, often indeed a more determining factor than the subject involved. States may apply to interstate trains a so-called "full crew law,"[32] but may not restrict the length of a freight train to seventy cars.[33] So the formula needs revision. A star Princeton football player who took my course at one Columbia University Summer Session once clarified the problem for us. He suggested that the nature of the subject is its nature after the regulation has been actually or hypothetically applied to it. Its nature is its situation or its characteristics after the state law has impinged upon it. This makes sense. It may well be what Mr. Justice Curtis had in mind, though he did not say it. The decision was not unanimous. Two Justices dissented, and a third preferred to sanction the law as one not essentially a regulation of commerce.

It seems clear that Mr. Justice Curtis thought that he was writing constitutional law, though he was aware that his law was not in the Constitution until he put it there. There were, however, some previous intimations before Mr. Justice Curtis. Webster, arguing in *Gibbons v. Ogden,* had distinguished between the higher and lower branches of the commerce power and had intimated that the higher were those which by their nature must be committed to a single hand.[34] Mr. Justice Woodbury seemed to think in the *License Cases* that the exclusive power is confined to the cases in which regulation {156} necessarily operates in more than one state.[35] This might ask for refinement. Not much state regulation "operates" outside the borders of the state, if "operates" means that the state forbids or commands conduct outside its borders. On the other hand, most state regulations of interstate transportation or interstate trade have effects in other states—have economic extraterritoriality though not legal external operation. State inspection laws are a familiar illustration.

If the Constitution, as officially interpreted in 1851, makes the commerce power of Congress an exclusive one over subjects for which a single uniform rule is preferable, it must be the Constitution that prohibits the states from exercising any commerce power over that type of commerce, as it prohibits the states from taxing the first sale of an import before bulk is broken. This does not necessarily mean that it is the Constitution that designates the so-called nature of each particular subject of commerce. It is the Court that does this designating in applying the Constitution. Ascertainment of the characteristic of physical things is essential to the judicial application of various canons and principles of both common law and public law, but it differs from the formulation of those canons and principles, even though it is true that their essential meaning is dependent in the long run on their applications. Reasonable time was not the same before the telegraph as afterwards; the law of percolating waters differed from what it was before enormous and powerful pumping machines came into use; ferries could be regarded as local in character in the horse and buggy days, {157} but they became national in character after the advent of the automobile.

What I am driving at may become clearer, perhaps even in my own mind, when considering state and national legislation on control of intoxicating liquor and theoretical difficulties in judicial lucubrations on constitutional powers in the premises. In 1888 the Supreme Court held in *Bowman v. Chicago and Northwestern R.R.*,[36] that a state may not forbid entrance of intoxicating liquor from another state, and in 1890 it held in *Leisy v. Hardin*[37] that a state may not forbid the first sale of liquor still in the original package shipped in from a sister state. These were deemed to be subjects national in character. Later Congress enacted the Wilson Act[38] allowing states to deal with liquor upon its arrival from outside as they deal with liquor of local origin. The Court held that "arrival" means arrival at its destination,[39] and therefore liquor got in to consignees. At Urbana, Illinois, there was a report that the expressman said to a consignee: "Professor, your box of books is leaking." The Wilson Act was followed by the Webb-Kenyon Act,[40] which, without imposing any penalty, forbade the interstate transportation of intoxicating liquor "intended by any person interested therein to be received, possessed, sold or in any manner used in violation of any law" of the state of destination.

After the first of these two Congressional statutes, the Court sustained state power to forbid the first sale[41] and, after the second, state power to forbid the intrusion of intoxicating liquor.[42] I have no difficulty with the {158} constitutionality of the federal statutes. They are both regulations of interstate commerce. My concern is with the theory by which the state laws can acquire constitutionality in the light of *Cooley v. Board of Port Wardens*.[43] If, as I assume, this case established that the national commerce power is split into two parts, one of which is exclusive of any similar state power, and the other of which is not, then decisions that state police power may not forbid the entrance or the first sale of intoxicants from beyond the state line must mean that the Constitution as officially interpreted is *pro tanto* a prohibition on state action. How then in any fashion can the states derive powers that the Constitution forbids them to exercise? The simplest way of course would be to rule that the Constitution permits Congress to delegate its power to the states, but this is denied by the Supreme Court. It was denied in the *Cooley* case.[44] Congress may adopt some state restrictions as its own, as it does with exemptions in bankruptcy, but it may not turn over national power to the states. They must in some theoretical fashion wield their own powers.

Another way out of the apparent hypothetical impasse is to say that the Court may yield in favor of Congress its earlier judicial judgment that the admission and sale of liquor are national in character and therefore require uniformity of regulation. This, however, by our assumption was a judicial judgment of constitutional law, though concededly it was judgment about a practical situation in the mere application of a constitutional canon. If Congress had made its judgment first, the Supreme Court out of deference might have accepted it. But is deference due to a Congressional {159} rejection of an earlier judicial judgment? Well, quite conceivably it may be, as in the case of the Wheeling bridge when a structure condemned by the Court acquired a new life when approved by Congress.[45] This caused difficulty as a possible legislative encroachment on judicial power, but the majority found the way to knuckle under. Such self-abasement is not a stimulus to judicial pride, and the Court in the Wilson and Webb-Kenyon cases did not avow that particular retreat.

Though Mr. Justice Curtis in the *Cooley* case treated his uniformity-diversity dichotomy as a characterization of the subject being regulated, it was not a judgment of any quality inherent in the subject. It was a determination of public policy as to wisdom in choosing between two possible ways of dealing with the subject, nationally or locally. For this reason, that great constitutional exegete, or may I say lexegete, James Bradley Thayer disapproved of the *Cooley* rule. His analysis was correct, but it does not follow that his judgment would be perennially wise, even though sufficiently satisfactory in simpler earlier seasons. His point is that the choice between uniformity and diversity of regulation is distinctly legislative in character. So it is. So also are judicial determinations in many fields of the law, where ethics, public policy, and other comparable considerations are components of their warp and woof. Mr. Thayer urged that "the courts should abstain from interference, except in cases so clear that the legislature cannot legitimately supersede its determinations; for the fact that the legislature may do this, in any given case, shows plainly that {160} the question is legislative and not judicial."[46] To me it does not follow that what in analysis is a judgment legislative in character, is therefore inappropriate for judicial consideration and determination. The issue seems to me a practical rather than a theoretical one, though I may be prejudiced in the premises because of some assigned brief-writing advocacy which was congenial to me and convincing to the Supreme Court.

Mr. Thayer is aware that Congress may be dilatory or negligent in considering the practical problems raised by Supreme Court tolerance toward all or most state impingements on the freedom of interstate transit and trade. His answer is that "the objection is a criticism upon the arrangements of the Constitution itself, in giving so much power to the legislature and so little to the courts." This might be acceptable if it were clear that the courts are guilty of usurpation in condemning debatable state obstructions to national concerns. This, however, is far from clear unless we should take the view that the judiciary must have explicit warrant in the Constitution for every exercise of claimed authority. Mr. Justice Black once averred that judicial condemnation of Arizona's train-limit law is a regulation of commerce and that this power of regulation was given to Congress and not to the courts.[47] Of course judicial negatives are regulations as much as legislative negatives are regulations. If these judicial negatives could be negatived only by constitutional amendment, the position would have practical wisdom. The {161} judicial affirmation of the power wielded by the Wilson and Webb-Kenyon Acts shows that there is relief other than by Constitutional amendment. Mr. Justice Black's theoretical argument suffers limitation when he concedes the judicial power to condemn state discriminations against interstate commerce.[48] This power is as self-assumed as is the power to condemn nondiscriminatory burdens.

I find no satisfying doctrinal justification for sanctioning Congressional resurrection of judicially expunged state liquor laws except by abandoning or modifying the constitutional conception of Mr. Justice Curtis. The clause he added to the fundamental law must not say that states are forbidden to regulate the commerce that is national in character and requires uniformity of regulation. It should emulate the restriction on the states reading that "No State shall, without the Consent of the Congress, lay any Imposts or Duties on Imports or Exports. . . ."[49] Such an alteration was indicated by Mr. Justice Matthews in the *Bowman* case and by Mr. Chief Justice Fuller in *Leisy v. Hardin,* when they spoke of what the state may not do except by "the express permission of Congress" or "in the absence of Congressional permission."[50] Thus the *Cooley* rule is not an absolute prohibition of state power over the commerce that is national in character, but only a qualified one. The states must leave national commerce alone unless by the consent of Congress. When Congress has not spoken, the states may deal with the commerce that admits of diversity of regulation but not with that which requires uniformity. {162} The Court has to determine in each case which type of commerce is involved, but it does so only to find out whether the Constitution leaves regulatory power to the states without the consent of Congress or forbids it without the consent of Congress.

This can keep the *Cooley* rule as a rule of constitutional interpretation, altering it only by making the prohibition on the states where it applies no longer absolute but one merely requiring the consent of Congress to lift it. A somewhat different alteration, but one leading to the same result, was also suggested by Mr. Justice Field in the *Bowman* case when, after saying that "where the subject is national in its character, and admits and requires uniformity of regulation, . . . Congress can alone act upon it and provide the needed regulations," he adds this significant fiat: "The absence of any law of Congress on the subject is equivalent to its declaration that commerce in that matter shall be free."[51] This is of course sheer make-believe, though not wholly lonely make-believe in the law, but it turns the *Cooley* rule from one of constitutional interpretation to one of legislative interpretation. I do not say "statutory interpretation," because *ex hypothesi* there is no statute to interpret. Hence the judicial exercise is often termed one of interpreting the silence of Congress.

By this judicial invention there is not constitutional division between concurrent and exclusive power over commerce. The power of Congress is concurrent with that of the states; the power of the states is concurrent with that of Congress. The exercise of state power, however, is subject to several restrictions. It must not impose regulation in conflict with {163} regulations of Congress. It must not, even in the absence of conflict, impose regulations if Congress, by what it has done, is deemed to have "occupied the entire field." A Congressional statute requiring grab irons on the ends and sides of freight cars, has been held to preclude the states from requiring them on the ends or sides of such cars. So a freight car with no grab irons at all was held not to violate the state law because it was inapplicable after Congress had dealt with the whole grab-iron matter.[52]

This is another form of legislation by silence. Marshall had praised a similar conception of counsel in *Gibbons v. Ogden* in favor of an exclusive power in Congress. The argument was that "regulation is designed for the entire result, applying to those parts which remain as they were, as well as to those which are altered." And, it continues, "It produces a uniform whole, which is as much disturbed and deranged by changing what the regulating power designs to leave untouched, as that on which it has operated."[53]

In sustaining the application of these state liquor laws after the two federal statutes, both Mr. Chief Justice Fuller and Mr. Chief Justice White prefer to call them exercises of the police power. I do not suppose that it matters much, but, in view of all the judicial talk about concurrent and exclusive commerce power for over a century, it seems to me better to recognize that it is a concurrent power in the field of commerce regulation that the state enjoys except when there are barriers to its exercise. Mr. Chief Justice Stone has not been afraid of writing of these state laws as regulations of commerce, both when condemned and when {164} sustained. In condemning a state train-limit law in application to interstate trains, where Congress had not dealt with the subject he said: "Whether or not this long-recognized distribution of power between the national and the state governments is predicated upon the implications of the commerce clause itself, . . . or upon the presumed intention of Congress, where Congress has not spoken, . . . the result is the same."[54] So it is where Congress has not spoken. But if one accepts the realistic position that these questioned state laws do really regulate commerce, it seems to me better to accept the view of a concurrent power, especially where the court applies a state law previously condemned because in the interim Congress has removed the bar to its earlier application.

In dealing with this name-calling contest, it is well to remember that in our constitutional federalism it is Congress and not the states which have power over interstate commerce *because* it is interstate commerce. Such powers as the states enjoy over such commerce derive *aliunde*, and the fact that interstate commerce is thereby regulated is a hurdle or a barrier rather than a justification. The judgment as to the height of the barrier and as to the desirability of being permitted to surmount it is not a judgment that the state is free to make as it chooses. Either the Court or Congress must make it. So multitudinous is the variety of the practical situations that must be assessed that it seems to me exceedingly unwise to apply a general rule that the states have no power or that they have all power until Congress acts. Whether the Justices of the Supreme Court are the individuals most competent to pass on questions of medicine, quarantine, {165} hydraulics, engineering and such, may be open to question. There are undoubtedly wider fields in which Congress might well adopt devices similar to that of requiring the consent of the Secretary of the Army to build bridges over the navigable waters of the United States.[55] The Secretary of the Army was chosen not because this was deemed primarily a military matter, but because the Department of the Army was equipped with an efficient Corps of Engineers.

The Wilson Act was entitled "An Act to limit the effect of the regulations of commerce between the several States and with foreign countries in certain cases."[56] The title of the Webb-Kenyon Act is "An Act Divesting intoxicating liquors of their interstate character in certain cases."[57] The latter title suggests a question. Is it not a constitutional matter when interstate commerce begins and ends? How may Congress say that it ends upon arrival at destination or that an interstate shipment may conditionally lose its interstate character? May Congress deny to any commodity the constitutional protection of the commerce clause, if that clause gives constitutional protection? These questions are somewhat loaded ones. The more satisfactory dogma now is that such protection as the Supreme Court gives to interstate commerce is the gift, not of the commerce clause, but of judicial divination of the meaning of Congressional silence. Moreover, Congress may not divest an interstate shipment of its interstate commerce character. It may only divest it of its legally protected interstate commerce character. Thus the barrier to state control is lifted.

I have spared you the pain of quotations from Mr. Chief {166} Justice White's opinion in *Clark Distilling Co. v. Western Maryland R. Co.*,[58] and if you should choose to read it or reread it, the burden is yours and not mine. A word, however, should be said about a bit of the opinion of Mr. Chief Justice Hughes in *Kentucky Whip & Collar Co. v. Illinois Central R.R.*[59] in sustaining the application of the Ashurst-Summers Act[60] to permit states to prevent the invasion of prison-made goods. Earlier similar effect had been given to the Hawes-Cooper Act,[61] modeled on the Wilson Act. This was in *Whitfield v. Ohio*,[62] in which a state was permitted to punish sale of prison-made goods in the original package in which they were shipped. Of the opinion in that case, Mr. Chief Justice Hughes said in the later case that "as it appeared that the Ohio statute would be unassailable if made to take effect after sale in the original package, the statute was held to be equally unassailable in the light of the provisions of the Hawes-Cooper Act."[63] This raises the interesting question whether without Congressional implementation the Supreme Court would in fact have permitted at that time a state to forbid a second sale, or sales in broken packages, because the goods were made by prison labor in another state.

Guessing about this requires analysis of *Baldwin v. G.A.F. Seelig, Inc.*,[64] which, two years before the *Kentucky Whip* case, condemned the application of a New York statute to a local sale of milk that had been bought in Vermont at a price to the producer which was less than the price required by New York to be paid to New York producers. {167} Such control by New York was essential if its minimum price requirements for New York-produced milk were to be saved from undercutting. It was new law to hold that the sale of broken packages, *i.e.*, of bottles filled from the shipping cans, is immune from state power—new, that is, unless the application of the New York statute to milk of Vermont origin might be deemed a discrimination against a product of extrastate origin. The Supreme Court's condemnation is not rested on the ground of discrimination as it could not well be, since milk from New York cows might not be sold in New York at that time if the producer had not been paid the stipulated minimum price. Some effort was made to regard the law as discriminatory because, it was suggested, extrastate milk needs a favorable differential because of extra cost of getting to market, and the absence of this differential might be thought to be discrimination against remote production, but this does not coincide with state lines. Connecticut is nearer to Manhattan than is Buffalo. So this immunity accorded to what is intrinsically a local sale needs some other justification.

It would be interesting to know whether the equalizing that New York sought and failed to secure by a prohibition on sale might be gained by an equalizing tax on the model of the use tax. Mr. Justice Cardozo, who likened the milk prohibition to a tariff, was the one who later wrote the opinion sustaining the use tax,[65] and there are declarations in the two opinions that savor somewhat of incongruity. The suggested tax would be one on sales of milk with a sufficient deduction so that tax plus price paid to the producer would be the same in all cases. Denial of a market by {168} prohibition is much more of an intrusion on a free national economy than is an equalizing tax. This was long ago recognized when the Court held that a state may tax,[66] but may not forbid,[67] a sale of products still in the original package in which they had entered from a sister state. The difference is emphasized now that an interstate sale is no longer wholly immune from a sales tax in the buyer's state.[68]

Another difference between the grasp of a tax and the grasp of a police measure finds illustration in disparate treatment of the question whether a sale is local or interstate. In *Lemke v. Fanners Grain Co.*[69] the Court denied the application of a North Dakota minimum price law to the sale of grain by North Dakota farmers for delivery to North Dakota grain elevators, calling the purchase interstate because the purchasers habitually and promptly shipped the grain to mills in Minnesota. Similarly, in *Dahnke-Walker Milling Co. v. Bondurant*,[70] a Kentucky law requiring registration of foreign corporations and exclusion of the unregistered from suit in the state courts was denied application to a suit by an extrastate unregistered corporate grain buyer which took delivery at the railroad station in the seller's state for shipment to Tennessee. By all the law I knew then or know now, these sales were local sales and subject to state taxation. A similar sale was held taxable in *Superior Oil Co. v. Mississippi*[71] subsequent to the two police power cases. I had a hard time distinguishing them {169} until it occurred to me that as in the state of destination, a sale of liquor in the original package in which it came from a sister state may not be prohibited but may be taxed, so in the state of origin, a price-fixing or registration requirement must keep farther away from the physical or contractual element of transportation than need a tax imposition.[72]

Taxation discriminating against interstate transportation or against extrastate production is seldom knowingly permitted, but some state police discrimination is found justifiable, and some is not. New Jersey was allowed to keep water from local streams for New Jersey consumption,[73] but West Virginia was not permitted to keep natural gas for West Virginia use.[74] Fish and game may be reserved for home acquisition and home consumption,[75] but a state may not ban the exit of shrimps from which the heads and hulls have not been removed.[76] The aim here was not home consumption but home processing and canning. Mr. Justice McReynolds thought that a state should be permitted to reserve a natural resource for economic purposes as well as for dietetic ones, but he was a dissenter, as often. The justifications {170} adduced for the discriminations sustained are sometimes based on ancient conceptions not originating in commerce clause situations, and I should think it preferable to invoke practical considerations if they can be found. Perhaps the difference between flowing water and natural gas may have a practical justification, but it was supported on what I am tempted to call irrelevant notions.

One of the practical reasons adduced by the Court against permitting the states, in the absence of Congressional sanction, to deal with intoxicants from sister states as they deal with home brew was that it would involve the Court in the multitudinous and perplexing tasks of drawing lines between many varieties of commodities that might meet with state disfavor. This, however, they let themselves in for when four years after *Leisy v. Hardin*[77] they differentiated oleomargarine colored to resemble butter from the beer they had protected.[78] Whether they learned something from the persistence of prohibitionists in starting us on the road to national interdiction, whether they preferred the National Grange to the WCTU, or whatever they thought, is not fully revealed. What they said was that it is fraudulent to color oleo to resemble butter, and the commerce clause does not protect fraud. Whether they would apply the same characterization to butter colored to resemble butter, as is so widely the practice, has not arisen for judgment. But in other instances the Court has condoned state legislation that serves in effect as a protective tariff on the cow,[79] though a halt was called against New York's effort to deny a market to Vermont's less expensive milk. {171}

Oleomargarine could hardly be put in the class of deleterious substances which are denied the protection of the commerce clause. With such substances states could hardly be denied power to deal effectively, since the Constitution assumes the perpetuation of state power to inspect and inevitably power to inspect must include power to reject on reasonable grounds. Quarantine laws excluding livestock from epidemic or infected areas are sustained when not deemed excessive,[80] though requirements assumed to be designed to curtail competition from sister states have been condemned.[81] Florida may keep green oranges at home in order to help preserve a good reputation for Florida citrus fruits that are not unripe and unfit for human consumption.[82] Protection of the original package is denied to meat falsely labeled Kosher.[83] A state may deny exit to large dead horses not slaughtered for food.[84] The exception permits the Faculty Club of Harvard University to acquire equine steaks for the sustenance of its members and guests. A lower federal court once sustained a tax of ten dollars required on removal of Chinese remains for shipment from California to the original homeland,[85] saying that a corpse is not an export. Thus the courts are compelled to make differentiations which illustrate the vagaries and varieties of constitutional interpretation.

Where the original package is still deemed a protection against the unfettered will of a state, there may be a question {172} as to what package is original. This arises more frequently in cases on state taxation of imports, but two have involved exercises of state police power against goods from sister states. Tennessee at one time forbade the sale of cigarettes, whether to protect the youth from coffin tacks or to give support to the widespread conviction that men of heroic mold take the weed in less combustible form, I do not know. Apparently upon legal advice, an extra-state manufacturer shipped in an open bushel basket a loose lot of small pasteboard packages, each containing a few cigarettes. He was denied constitutional protection.[86] So later he or someone else dispensed with the basket and piled the small pasteboard packages on the floor of the express car. He too failed in his constitutional hopes.[87] Whether the Court deemed the basket or the car floor the shipping case or thought that it was only normal commercial shipping methods that are entitled to protection, is not wholly clear. Both ideas are at least adumbrated. There are other instances in constitutional law in which the Court has seemed to disrelish reliance on their judicial distinctions in what I call "You think you're smart" cases. So far as I know, this refinement has not been applied to state taxation of foreign imports. Without contest, hundred-pound bags of nitrate were held to be imports, though they were quite suitable for retail sale.[88]

Since the several states may take measures to ensure that the intrinsic qualities of commodities are safe and sound and meet representations, it would seem almost a corollary that they may take other measures to safeguard the performance {173} of interstate contracts, such as repairing the registration of extrastate vendors so they may be subject to suit or requiring the giving of a bond conditioned on fulfillment of voluntarily assumed obligations in seeking to make money from local vendees. Such provisions have, however, had a hard row to hoe with the Supreme Court. It seemed rather rough that ambitious residents induced to take courses by correspondence from extrastate concerns with solicitors in Kansas could not have assurances that the promises would be duly fulfilled. Yet the device of precluding the vendor from suing in the Kansas courts if it had not registered so that it might be sued there was condemned.[89] Doubtless the state's slamming of the door against suit by the non-registered was too drastic, but with my disrelish of soliciting vendors I would welcome some way to make them defendants where by a judicial dictate they must have a right to be plaintiffs.

Just how far any modification of the *Correspondence School* case has gone, I do not know, now that I no longer page the Supreme Court reports as I did for some hundred and fifty years—years not of my time but of the career of the reports. *Union Brokerage Co. v. Jensen*[90] in 1944 sanctioned such exclusion as was condemned in the *Textbook* case, but this would-be plaintiff was a customs brokerage concern wholly confined in its activities to the regulating state, and its action was against a defaulting employee and not on an interstate transaction, although its own business was con-fined to handling the details of securing entrance and clearance of goods imported from abroad by its clients. {174} Automobilists on interstate journeys may be made to halt at the state border and get a license,[91] as they may be made subject to suit by service on the Secretary of State.[92] I do not cotton greatly to the adduced justification of the proprietary power of the state over the highways or to that of the promotion of safety. I doubt if any motorist looks up the law of any state he enters, and drives carefully where he is subject to suit and carelessly where he is not. I think that there is as much justification for suit against a fly-by-night escaped vendor as for suit against a migrant motorist. If the vendor retains a sufficient staff of solicitors within the states, it is subject to service of process.[93] I would sustain court jurisdiction on causes of action arising from business done within the state even if it was former interstate business that has wholly ceased.

Traditional principles that a state may not require a license to do in-terstate or foreign commerce were applied brusquely and mechanically by Mr. Justice Butler in *Di Santo v. Pennsylvania*[94] to relieve brokers of steamship tickets, not agents of the steamship companies, from a re-quirement to take out a license, pay fifty dollars, and give a bond to in-demnify persons who suffer from defaults in carrying out their assurances.

Mr. Justice Brandeis wrote a dissenting opinion along rather traditional lines, saying that the effect on commerce was indirect and invoking the cases sustaining state requirements on the operation of interstate trains. Mr. Justice Stone wrote a separate dissent, {175} pointing out that "direct" and "indirect" were labels for results rather than outlines of substantial justifications for them. He gave substantial reasons. Mr. Justice Brandeis concurred in the Stone dissent and Mr. Justice Holmes concurred in both of them. In his own opinion Mr. Justice Brandeis justified departure from previous cases, saying: "Each case required the decision of the question of law. Each involved merely an appreciation of the facts. Neither involved the declaration of a rule of law."[95] His rule of law was merely the power of the state to impose indirect burdens, but not direct ones. The cup is empty until filled with practical details.

The *Di Santo* case survived less than fifteen years. Mr. Chief Justice Stone was its executioner in *California v. Thompson*.[96] The fee for filing there was only one dollar and the required bond was for $1,000. The former Dean of the Columbia Law School told me after his *Di Santo* dissent that he was disturbed that the fee was as high as fifty dollars. But in *Robertson v. California*,[97] which followed the *Thompson* case, the fee for what is called a surplus-line broker was fifty dollars and the bond was for $5,000. Such fees may not be imposed as mere fiscal measures but so far as I recall, we have had no cases in the Supreme Court where regulatory provisions were held to be a mere pretense to deceive the Court. Of course all these concerns subject to the license and bond requirements were doing continuous business within the state through solicitors and perhaps other employees. It would take regulation by Congress to supervise the conduct of the enterprises which remain wholly outside the state in which by advertising they {176} solicit interstate business. The state of their headquarters seldom seeks to prescribe rules for conduct in other states, and faces issues of extraterritoriality when its general requirements are sought to be applied in a sister state. The home state may have little desire to protect victimized external vendees. Such vendees would at any rate usually have to go to the vendor's state to sue.

From this cursory review it is evident that the later trend in Supreme Court adjudications is to sanction state action when from the standpoint of practical considerations it interferes with the national economy no more than is deemed to be justified by the importance of the resulting protection of community interests. Both sides of the scale must be given consideration. Even when Congress has acted, there is now more opportunity than formerly for state complementary action. In *Parker v. Brown*,[98] the State of California required producers of raisins to market part of their crop through a Program Committee, although 90 percent of the California crop was shipped to points outside. The law was held to be not in conflict with the Sherman Act and not in conflict with Congressional marketing legislation, because it was in accord with the national legislative policy applied to various other crops. Such a decision would hardly have been possible in the days of more mechanically minded doctrinarians. This newer attitude is not judicial surrender. Where the burden on commerce is adjudged too heavy to be justified by the service to any genuine state need, there will be condemnation, as is manifest by *Southern Pacific Co. v. Arizona*[99] which denied enforcement to a state law limiting freight-train length to seventy cars, differentiating it {177} from so-called full-crew laws and other requirements which states have been allowed to apply to interstate train service.

One still recognized objection to state legislation is that against discrimination against interstate trade in favor of local enterprise. A recent illustration is found in *Dean Milk Co. v. City of Madison*[100] condemning an ordinance forbidding the sale of any milk as pasteurized unless processed and bottled in an approved plant within five miles of the central square of the city. Mr. Justice Clark declared that reasonable and adequate alternatives are available. So also the Supreme Court thought in *Minnesota v. Barber*[101] in 1890, when they felt enough confidence in inspection by sister states and so condemned a statute requiring as a prerequisite to sale of meat products an inspection within twenty-four hours prior to slaughter. This statute would increase interstate transportation of live animals but not of those no longer on the hoof. How well other states could be trusted to apply adequate inspection was revealed in Upton Sinclair's *The Jungle,* which contributed to the enactment of the Federal Pure Food and Drug Act.[102] One of the latest state preference statutes to fall by the wayside was a phase of the milk regulation of New York, condemned in *Hood & Sons, Inc. v. Du Mond.*[103] This sought to restrict further receiving facilities for obtaining and processing milk. Its application was contested by a Massachusetts distributor which desired to increase its New York supply. New York's desire to favor the home market was frustrated by the Court.

These varying instances of practical judgments could be {178} multiplied by hundreds. A village of 800 population which was a county seat could in 1897 require train service[104] the Court would not accord in 1923 to a community of 2,500 with a State Poultry Experiment Station.[105] The state of origin may not prescribe how a telegram shall be delivered in a sister state,[106] but that destination sister may do so.[107] Considerations of extraterritoriality, economic as well as legal, are elements taken account of. So after my students had searched in vain for a formula, I suggested that one might safely say that the states may regulate commerce some, but not too much. Of course there are subordinate criteria, but many of them pull judgment in opposite directions. Once I asked Mr. Justice Holmes why counsel should not give up prating about national and local, uniformity and diversity, and tell the court that the law is free for a decision either way, and then add: "I propose to confine myself to practical considerations why my way is wiser than my opponent's way." He remarked: "I wish to God they would." But the Justices have led the way in what, after you have fathomed it and weighed its applications, you may be tempted to call folderol. But their doctrines as modified in recent years have not been unduly constrictive. They have various verbal capsules containing a variety of prescriptions. One of the most elastic is that this or that state action does not regulate commerce but merely incidentally affects it, or, even if it regulates, it does so only indirectly.

As I reflect on the animadversions I have been casting {179} from the memory of many years of teaching in hopes of inducing students to think things instead of words, I wonder if I have been too dogmatic, too caustic, too critical. Of course I have been selective in choosing my illustrations. I have been arguing a thesis, as lawyers usually do. So now by way of caveat, let me say that I do not contend that any type of thinking or of behaving is universal or without exceptions even among individual Justices. I think that what I most object to in many Justices is something that springs from a feeling of judicial duty to try to make out that their conclusions come from the Constitution. True it is that so far as state laws are involved, the task of passing on them in the field of commerce comes from the Constitution. The performance, however, comes mainly from the judges, and on the whole it has created for us a fairly well balanced constitutional federalism. For me it has been a fascinating field for study and for teaching. The intricacies and varieties in reasoning and results have provided for us much food for thought, and not a little food for lawyers. Even this professor who gave up advocacy for thinking, as he thought, has occasionally gathered manna from the judicial Heaven.

Notes

1 9 Wheat. 1.

2 U.S. CONST., ART. VI.

3 Johnson, J. concurring, 9 Wheat. 1, 222, 231-33.

4 Ogden v. Gibbons, 4 Johns. Ch. 150 & 174 (N.Y., 1819), *aff'd* 17 Johns. 488 (N.Y., 1820).

5 Willson v. Black Bird Creek Marsh Co., 2 Pet. 245 (1829).

6 9 Wheat. at 209.

7 *Id.* at 210.

8 *Id.* at 203.

9 *Supra* n. 5.

10 2 Pet. at 251 and 252.

11 9 Wheat. at 204-5.

12 3 Wall. 713.

13 *Id.* at 732.

14 Pennsylvania v. Wheeling & Belmont Bridge Co., 13 How. 518 (1852).

15 3 Wall, at 729.

16 95 U.S. 485, 491, 515 (1878).

17 8 Pet. 120, 122 (1834).

18 9 Pet. 85 (1835).

19 11 Pet. 102.

20 *Id.* at 158.

21 15 Pet. 449.

22 5 How. 504 (1847).

23 12 Wheat. 419 (1827).

24 1 Cr. 137 (1803). With Reverdy Johnson, Taney had argued *Brown v. Maryland* on behalf of the State.

25 Hooven & Allison Co. v. Evatt, 324 U.S. 652 (1945).

26 Scott v. Sandford, 19 How. 393 (1857).

27 5 How. at 601.

28 7 How. 283 (1849).

29 12 How. 299.

30 *Id.* at 319.

31 *Id.* at 320.

32 Chicago, R.I. & P.R. Co. v. Arkansas, 219 U.S. 453 (1911); Missouri Pacific R. Co. v. Norwood, 283 U.S. 249 (1931).

33 Southern Pacific Co. v. Arizona, 325 U.S. 761 (1945).

34 See 9 Wheat. 1, 9, 13-14, and *passim.*

35 5 How. at 624-25. See also Woodbury, J. in the Passenger Cases, 7 How. at 559-61.

36 125 U.S. 465.

37 135 U.S. 100.

38 26 STAT. 313 (1890).

39 Rhodes v. Iowa, 170 U.S. 412 (1898).

40 37 STAT. 699 (1913).

41 *In re* Rahrer, 140 U.S. 545 (1891).

42 Clark Distilling Co. v. Western Maryland Ry., 242 U.S. 311 (1917).

43 *Supra* n. 29.

44 12 How. at 318.

45 Pennsylvania v. Wheeling & Belmont Bridge Co., 18 How. 421 (1856).

46 2 THAYER, CASES ON CONSTITUTIONAL LAW 2191 (Cambridge, 1895).

47 See Black, J., concurring in Morgan v. Virginia, 328 U.S 373, 386-87 (1946), where reference is made, *inter alia*, to Southern Pacific Co. v. Arizona, 325 U.S. 761 (1945). See dissent of Black, J. in this case, 325 U.S. at 784 *et seq.*

48 *See, e.g.,* dissent in Hood v. Du Mond, 336 U.S. 525, 545, 549, 555-57 (1949).

49 U.S. CONST., ART. I, § 10.

50 125 U.S. at 485; 135 U.S. at 124.

51 125 U.S. at 507-8.

52 Southern Ry. v. RR. Comm. of Indiana, 236 U.S. 439 (1915).

53 9 Wheat, at 209.

54 325 U.S. at 768.

55 33 U.S.C. §§491, 525.

56 26 STAT. 313 (1890).

57 37 STAT. 699 (1913).

58 242 U.S. 311 (1917).

59 299 U.S. 334 (1937).

60 49 STAT. 494 (1935).

61 45 STAT. 1084 (1929).

62 297 U.S. 431 (1936).

63 299 U.S. at 351.

64 294 U.S. 511 (1935).

65 Henneford v. Silas Mason Company, 300 U.S. 577 (1937).

66 Woodruff v. Parham, 8 Wall. 123 (1869).

67 Leisy v. Hardin, 135 U.S. 100 (1890).

68 McGoldrick v. Berwind-White Coal Mining Co., 309 U.S. 33 (1940); Norton Co. v. Dept. of Revenue, 340 U.S. 534 (1951).

69 258 U.S. 50 (1922).

70 257 U.S. 282 (1921).

71 280 U.S. 390 (1930).

72 It may be that the need for the suggested distinction no longer exists. Milk Control Board v. Eisenberg Farm Products, 306 U.S. 346 (1939) possibly, and Cities Service Gas Co. v. Peerless Oil & Gas Co., 340 U.S. 179 (1950) more probably, have indicated that the *Lemke* and *Dahnke-Walker* cases may no longer have great authority. In turn, it may be of interest to note that the *Cities Service* decision may well have suffered statutory, though probably not constitutional, eclipse by virtue of Phillips Petroleum Co. v. Wisconsin, 347 U.S. 672 (1954).

73 Hudson Water Co. v. McCarter, 209 U.S. 349 (1908).

74 Pennsylvania v. West Virginia, 262 U.S. 553 (1923).

75 McCready v. Virginia, 94 U.S. 391 (1876); Geer v. Connecticut, 161 U.S. 519 (1896).

76 Foster-Fountain Packing Co. v. Haydel, 278 U.S. 1 (1928). *Cf.* Toomer v. Witsell, 334 U.S. 385 (1948).

77 *Supra* n. 67.

78 Plumley v. Massachusetts, 155 U.S. 461 (1894).

79 See Mintz v. Baldwin, 289 U.S. 346 (1933), and *cf.* TAYLOR, BURTIS AND WAUGH, BARRIERS TO INTERNAL TRADE IN FARM PRODUCTS 93 (Washington, 1939).

80 Smith v. St. Louis & S.W.R. Co. 181 U.S. 248 (1901). *Cf.* Mintz v. Baldwin, *supra* n. 79.

81 Railroad Co. v. Husen, 95 U.S. 465 (1878).

82 Sligh v. Kirkwood, 237 U.S. 52 (1915).

83 Hygrade Provision Co. v. Sherman, 266 U.S. 497 (1925).

84 Clason v. Indiana, 306 U.S. 439 (1939).

85 *In re* Wong Yung Quy, 2 Fed. 624 (C.C., D. Calif., 1880).

86 Austin v. Tennessee, 179 U.S. 343 (1900).

87 Cook v. Marshall County, 196 U.S. 261 (1905).

88 Anglo-Chilean Nitrate Sales Corp. v. Alabama, 288 U.S. 218 (1933).

89 International Textbook Co. v. Pigg, 217 U.S. 91 (1910).

90 322 U.S. 202.

91 Kane v. New Jersey, 242 U.S. 160 (1916).

92 Hess v. Pawloski, 274 U.S. 352 (1927). *Cf.* Wuchter v. Pizzutti, 276 U.S. 13 (1928).

93 International Shoe Co. v. Washington, 326 U.S. 310 (1945).

94 273 U.S. 34 (1927).

95 *Id.* at 42.

96 313 U.S. 109 (1941).

97 328 U.S. 440 (1946).

98 317 U.S. 341 (1943).

99 *Supra* n. 33.

100 340 U.S. 349 (1951).

101 136 U.S. 313.

102 34 STAT. 768 (1906); 34 STAT. 1260 (1907).

103 336 U.S. 525 (1949).

104 Gladson v. Minnesota, 166 U.S. 427.

105 St. Louis-San Francisco Ry. v. Public Service Comm., 261 U.S. 369.

106 Western Union Tel. Co. v. Pendleton, 122 U.S. 347 (1887).

107 Western Union Tel. Co. v. James, 162 U.S. 650 (1896).

VI. Federalism: State Powers
Affecting the National Economy;
State Taxing Power

TAXATION is regulation. The states may not tax interstate and foreign commerce, hereinafter called commerce. Such were the short and simple annals of Supreme Court dogma on the subject for a long period.[1] The test of validity is the subject taxed, by which is meant the legal subject taxed, not generally the economic effect of the tax,[2] though there are a few exceptions. There is no *Cooley* rule[3] governing state taxation. If the subject is commerce, there is no consideration of local or national, uniformity or diversity. Those are police power formulae, not canons of state taxing power. At one time, however, the distinction bade fair to intrude into the taxing field. It was held that commerce in gas and electricity is interstate from the outside well or generator to the jet and the lamp, provided there is no intervention of a middleman distributor. But the rates at jet and lamp were held to be local in character and so fit for diversity of regulation.[4] This suggested the issue whether {181} the gross receipts paid by the consumer would be held subject to state taxation. Happily the issue was avoided by a change in theory. When pressure was stepped down or voltage reduced, there came a break in the interstate transmission, and the rest of the service became intrastate.[5]

This break in the transmission was likened to the breaking of the original package in Marshall's dividing line in *Brown v. Maryland*.[6] This case involved a state tax on selling imported goods at wholesale. The tax discriminated against selling goods of foreign origin, but Marshall did not base condemnation on that ground. He held that the constitutional ban on state taxation of imports keeps the state from subjecting them to a general non-discriminatory tax, so long as they remain imports. This opens the question when they cease to be imports. The answer was that they remain imports until after the first sale or after bulk has been broken by opening the shipping case and extracting some of the contents.[7] So far as I know, the removal of one pasteboard box from the wooden shipping case ends

121

the immunity of the other pasteboard boxes still left in the traveling container. The Supreme Court has never told me this, but it has never told me anything to the contrary. It has told me that if all the inner pasteboard boxes have been taken out and put on a retailer's shelves, they have all ceased to be imports.[8]

Marshall reached his condemnation of Maryland's occupation tax by invocation of the commerce clause as well as the ban against taxing imports. He considers whether the power of Congress is exclusive of state power to tax and {182} has some statements that by themselves would indicate that he so thinks, but he intersperses others that by themselves might be taken otherwise.[9] This uncertainty is rendered harmless for the disposition of the particular case, for the technical ground of the decision on the commerce clause is that Congress by its customs regulations had already acted so as to preclude state taxation so long as the import remains an import. This is as questionable as was Marshall's invocation of the Coasting License in *Gibbons v. Ogden*.[10] Moreover it was an adventure in supererogation to wield the club of the commerce clause for a second lethal blow after the import clause had successfully committed legicide. It was altogether *obiter*, also, to conclude by saying that: "It may be proper to add, that we suppose the principles laid down in this case, to apply equally to importations from a sister State."[11]

Though I might question whether it was proper thus to add something not called for by the case, I certainly would have agreed that goods from sister states are imports. When the Framers spoke in 1787, the states were substantially sovereign, and their exercises of sovereign powers in adversely affecting trade from sister states was one of the factors leading to the Annapolis conference which on its un-success made the recommendation eventuating in the Philadelphia convention of 1787. Nevertheless, forty years after Marshall's dictum, the Supreme Court held in *Woodruff v. Parham*[12] that only goods from foreign countries are to be deemed imports. Mr. Justice Miller proffers historical and literary support for this conclusion in a passage which I {183} have always found confusing when I glanced at it, and which I have, *mea culpa*, never taken the time to evaluate. He also seeks to shove the actual result of *Brown v. Maryland* aside by saying that the tax there was discriminatory against foreign goods and that the same condemnation would apply to such discrimination against goods from sister states,[13] but Marshall himself did not invoke discrimination.

Whatever confidence or lack of confidence Mr. Justice Miller may have had in his venture into verbiage and history, he makes it clear that he is dominated by considerations of practical desirability and undesirability. His judgment might be taken as an adverse comment on Marshall's grant of immunity to imports after arrival and before sale, but Mr. Justice Miller might still have made a distinction between goods from abroad and goods from sister states, as in a number of ways his successors have. At any rate, as to the latter, after asserting his conclusion he adds: "If we examine for a moment the results of an opposite doctrine, we shall be well satisfied with the wisdom of the Constitution as thus construed."[14] In other words, he put in his thumb and pulled out a plum and said "What a good boy am I." The wisdom he elaborates as follows:

> The merchant of Chicago who buys his goods in New York and sells at wholesale in the original packages, may have his millions employed in trade for half a lifetime and escape all State, county, and city taxes; for all that he is worth is invested in goods which he claims to be protected as imports from New York. Neither the State nor the city which protects his life and property can make him contribute a dollar to {184} support its government, improve its thoroughfares or educate its children. The merchant in a town in Massachusetts, who deals only in wholesale, if he purchase his goods in New York, is exempt from taxation. If his neighbor purchase in Boston, he must pay all the taxes which Massachusetts levies with equal justice on the property of all citizens.[15]

This seems not a little extravagant, at least as far as property taxation is concerned. Tax day, like Christmas, comes but once a year. Much merchandise will be received and sold between assessment dates. The retail merchant sells most of his stock after opening the shipping case. This is induced by desire for display and for convenience in delivery. Mr. Justice Miller's dire predictions would have more force if goods from sister states were so sold as to be immune from a sales tax or an occupation tax like that in *Brown v. Maryland*. The tax in *Woodruff v. Parham* was a sales tax, but at least some of the sales were sales at auction which Marshall expressly excepted from his canon of immunity for imports.[16] Mr. Justice Miller's failure to premise immunity on this specialized differentiation of sales at auction indicates the conviction of the majority that goods from sister states should lose their immunity from taxation upon arrival at their destination, a position directly in contrast with their continuing protection from drastic exercises of the police power.[17]

This subjection of goods from sister states to taxation upon arrival at their destination was reaffirmed in *Brown v. Houston*[18] in 1885. Coal from Pennsylvania was held taxable {185} in Louisiana while still on the flatboats which brought it down-river to New Orleans. Had the coal come from Wales, it would not yet have become intermingled with the common mass of property in the state.[19] Coming from Pennsylvania, it was so intermingled. When it is intermingled, it is taxable. When not intermingled, it is immune. When it is immune, it is not intermingled. When it is taxable, the intermingling is obvious. It all depends upon where the coal came from. The cart can follow as well as precede the horse, and precede as well as follow.

These two cases are law today, but for a season they got strangely lost in the shuffle. In 1898, *Patapsco Guano Co. v. North Carolina Board of Agriculture*[20] sustained an inspection fee on fertilizer from sister states upon the finding that the levy was not substantially in excess of the cost of inspection. Similar inspection fees were sustained for the same reason.[21] Evidently the reason operated to develop in the judicial head a negative pregnant. So in some later cases, inspection fees deemed excessive were condemned even when charged on sales negotiated after the commodities were within the state.[22] At the same time, however, an occupation tax was sustained on a soft drink business in which the vendor crossed the state line in the absence of orders but in hopes of purchase by regular customers,[23] much as {186} a milkman finds from the empty bottles or a note what the customer will take on each trip. The only acceptable distinction between these cases is that one involved ginger ale and the others involved gasoline. For a season it was uncertain whether the gasoline principle or the ginger ale principle would prevail, if both could not continue in amity.

It all got straightened out in *Sonneborn v. Cureton*[24] in 1923, in which *Woodruff v. Parham* and *Brown v. Houston* were restored to unquestioned standing so that now, as earlier, sales made after arrival must contribute to the public fisc. In the *Sonneborn* case Mr. Chief Justice Taft conceded that there were "observations in the opinions which unless much restricted in their application constitute a departure from theretofore established principles."[25] This indicates that there may have been errors of law, yet he says also that the facts "do not appear fully in any of the cases, or to have been discussed by counsel."[26] If the Court had been certain about the law, they might have been more inquisitive about the facts. The *Sonneborn* case affirms taxability only of sales made after arrival. Its opinion still respected the immunity of genuine interstate sales, *i.e.*, sales of goods ordered from sister states and shipped in to the purchaser in fulfillment of the order or contract of acceptance.[27]

After the *Sonneborn* opinion, it was an apparently reliable assumption that interstate sales—genuine interstate sales—were immune from taxation either by the state of the buyer or by the state of the seller. It is true that the leading case on the point was *Robbins v. Shelby County Taxing District*[28] which in 1887 condemned a privilege tax on drummers {187} who solicited within the District orders for goods at that time outside the state. This was a specific anticipatory license fee. Such a fee cannot be measured by volume or gross receipts or net income, because the fee is due before orders are solicited. If the college student may not in his vacation solicit orders for magazines or vacuum cleaners or anything else to be shipped in from beyond the state without having to pay an anticipatory fixed fee in every town and village where he wishes to make his annoying calls, he is likely to be restrained from the effort by any fiscal exaction other than the merest minimum. Hence, in spite of increasing judicial tolerance toward various forms of economic burdens on interstate sales, *Nippert v. Richmond*[29] in 1946 follows *Robbins v. Shelby County Taxing District* in condemning a specific anticipatory license fee for soliciting victims to give orders for extrastate goods.

There have long been questions whether a particular order is for extrastate goods. An automobile dealer may make a sale deemed local though he does not buy from the extra-state manufacturer until after he gets the order.[30] On the other hand, orders to be filled C.O.D. are interstate though title does not pass until payment within the buyer's state.[31] A solicitor may get separate orders for a dozen brooms, have them shipped in together, and not allocate a particular broom to a particular lady until, after arrival, the bundle is opened, but the purchases are nevertheless interstate.[32] Place of contracting and place of payment are not determinative, {188} for these may be rigged to favor immunity.[33] There are dozens of variations in the dealings that give rise to such issues between local and interstate, and until the advent of sales and gross receipts taxes the decisions were fairly consistent with only an occasional sport or two.

Then ensued a few cases which seemed out of line with what had gone before. These involved gross receipts taxes. Though in 1938 and 1939 the Court condemned gross receipts taxes in the state of the vendor on interstate sales,[34] the majority of the Justices had begun to find some new reasons for agreeing with the buyer's state that the sale was really local. One such reason was that the seller would not violate his contract if he filled the order from stock within the state instead of from stock outside.[35] Always before the test had been whether the order was in fact filled from stock in a sister state, provided it was not a situation in which the local vendor to a local vendee himself had become a vendee from an extrastate vendor to get the commodity to make his sale. Even then delivery could perhaps be telescoped by request to the outside shipper to ship directly to his vendee's vendee. Doubtless by this changed analysis of what makes a local sale we should have been forewarned that the Court was getting ready to go still further and to permit the state of the buyer to impose a sales tax on sales concededly interstate.

This is what happened in *McGoldrick v. Berwind-White Coal Mining Co.*[36] In 1940, over the dissent of Mr. Chief {189} Justice Hughes and Justices McReynolds and Roberts, who preferred not to forget the ancient landmarks. Mr. Justice Stone for the majority was somewhat happier in supporting the wisdom of the result than in finding it warranted by previous decisions. He said that "we have sustained the tax where the course of business and the agreement for sale plainly contemplated the shipment interstate in fulfilment of the contract."[37] This was true enough, but the cases cited in support[38] were cases in which the Court at the time chose to call the sales not ones in interstate commerce. Such things have happened before in constitutional law. First a differentiation and perhaps several more. Then a discounting of the differentiation to shift the underpinning to what it should originally have been conceded to be. New wine in old bottles followed by new bottles for old wine.

One would have to be unduly myopic not to perceive the undoubted need of the state of the market for protection from the competition of untaxed deliveries of goods from sister states. In response to this need came the so-called use taxes, in terms applicable to the first use of various commodities without differentiation as to the source of acquisition, except that any sales tax paid to the purchaser's state might be deducted from the use tax, reducing the assessment for the latter to zero where a sales tax had been paid upon purchase.

Use taxes were sustained on the theory that the use could not begin until after delivery, thus completing any interstate purchase. The complaint of discrimination against the {190} use of commodities acquired in or from a sister state was rejected by marrying together the sales and the use tax so that in one form or the other the burden was the same whatever the nature of the sale. What Mr. Justice Cardozo had said about a tariff in condemning New York's treatment of Vermont's underpriced milk made it appropriate to assign to him the leading opinion sustaining use taxes, but his skill was adequate for the task, or nearly so.[39] Once the use tax device was sanctioned, it would have seemed unduly nominalistic not to have allowed the tax to impinge upon the interstate sale rather than on the subsequent use. One may of course perceive dangers to interstate trade if use taxes are not given credit for some exactions by the seller's state, particularly if that exaction were in name as well as in fact a tax on the sale to the buyer in the sister state.

This particular menace has been forfended by the Supreme Court's condemnation of a tax on an interstate sale levied by the seller's state. In *Freeman v. Hewit*[40] in 1946, Mr. Justice Frankfurter was rather formal in condemning the tax as one on the sale itself, since from that aspect it can hardly be differentiated from the tax in the buyer's state, but the result seems acceptable even if the clearest justification is not one easy to elaborate in a judicial opinion. The evil of sales taxes on interstate sales lay in the possibility that the state at the beginning and the state at the end of the transaction might each impose a tax, whereas intrastate sales would be subject to but one assessment. So the earlier notion was that no tax was better than two. It was Mr. Justice {191} Stone who led the way in emphasizing the practicalities of the problem. The solution by the judgment of Solomon has not yet been worked out in the form of cutting the tax in two and giving half to each state.[41] It might well take national action and administration to emulate Solomon's wisdom.

The danger of economic duplication would not be avoided if a local purchase in the seller's state were succeeded by use in the buyer's state and if under different names two taxes were levied. This might raise the question of which state is the more to blame for participation in the duplication. The state of the buyer needs protection of its finances and of its local merchants from undercutting by tax differentials in favor of interstate or extrastate sales. But by our hypothesis of the moment, there is no undercutting if there are double or bistate burdens. The state of the seller is unlikely to desire to burden its commerce toward sister states unless it has secure competitive advantages. On the other hand, it needs revenue. It can get such revenue by taxes impinging on incidents prior to the sale.[42] So comparisons between burdens on intrastate and interstate trade ought to take account of the totality of burdens, and I for one do not know how to do it. It may be enough to pretermit further inquiry or analysis by taking comfort in the fact that somehow or other we seem to be getting on fairly well in our manufacturing and merchandising across and within state boundaries.

From the standpoint of public finance, one aspect of {192} taxation is the problem of collection. The Supreme Court has held that a seller of extrastate supplies who has a sufficient establishment in the market state may be required to pay a sales tax[43] and to collect a use tax.[44] Without such sufficient establishment in the market state, he may not be compelled to pay a sales tax,[45] but he still may be obliged to collect and pay over a use tax.[46] The difference between the two rulings seems to me indefensible. The seller is closer to the sale than he is to the use. I should take the view either that both cases should go the same way or that each of them should have gone the other way. Six Justices thought that both cases should go the same way, but they did not agree on the way they ought to go. Of one thing at least, I am quite sure. It does not satisfy me at all to justify the obligation of the remote and alien seller to collect and pay over a use tax by saying no more than that this is a familiar and sanctioned device. So it is, if an extra-state seller has a sufficient leverage in the buyer's state. But if he has not enough there to make him liable for a sales tax, how has he enough to make him a collector of a use tax?[47] Of course he may often escape by being out of reach. {193}

When the issue first arose clearly, the Supreme Court held that taxes on net incomes are not forbidden burdens on interstate or foreign commerce.[48] The main bone of contention here is one of allocating to the taxing state its respectable share of net income from multistate operations.[49] The problems are fascinating, but they do not seem to me distinctly commerce clause issues as much as they are intrinsically due process ones, though bigger interests are at stake if the commerce clause may be invoked. Many of these complaints are now often soothed by administrative grace, hence the contemporary Supreme Court gets few of them. It has held that an allocation may not be upset merely by showing an error in the application of one of several factors.[50] This may be counterbalanced by contrasting infelicity in other factors. So a complainant must establish evil in the end result of the figuring. I have known of an instance where a taxpayer chose not to be too explicit for fear he would reveal to a sister state that her demand was unduly moderate.

The vice of the assessment of extraterritorial values is one {194} that caused a doctrinal upset that many observers found most perplexing. In *Western Union Telegraph Co. v. Kansas*,[51] in 1910, a majority of the Supreme Court condemned an excise on doing local business for the vice of being measured by total capital stock representing values preponderantly outside the state. The underlying basis of the decision should have been clear enough as soon as the Court sustained other excises measured by that portion of the capital representing property and business in the taxing state.[52] But what of the doctrine? The subject taxed was doing local business, a wholly proper subject. The property was not taxed. It was only used as a measure. If exempt United States bonds or the interest thereon may be the measure of a privilege tax, why not extraterritorial assets? There certainly was doctrinal discrepancy enough. Yet this assessment of extraterritorial assets as a measure and not a subject might have been condemned as *Welton v. Missouri*[53] condemned a tax on local sales because it applied only to sales of articles with an extrastate past. It should, however, be recognized that the majority Justices in the *Western Union* case were not too clear about the new law they were making, and it was far from clear how far the new law was going to go.

Some special grounds for the decision in the *Western Union* case were ones that would not be equally applicable to a manufacturing corporation,[54] and some Massachusetts taxes actually measured by total capital stock representing {195} values partly within but chiefly beyond the Commonwealth were later upheld because of a provision in the statute setting a $2,000 maximum to the annual demand.[55] And this, though the rate of the levy was such that the maximum would not avail any corporation with a capital of less than ten million dollars. If the Supreme Court did not fully understand what it was doing, and if Justices who agreed in results did not agree in doctrine or in justification, it is not surprising that outsiders, including judges of state courts, should be perplexed. Judge Henshaw of the California Supreme Court, an able lawyer, wrote the following lament for our sympathy:

We are constrained to admit our inability to harmonize this language and these decisions, though we make haste to add that undoubtedly the failure must come from our own deficient powers of perception and ratiocination, and for this deficiency it is no consolation to us to note that our brethren of the Supreme Court of Montana are similarly afflicted. . . .[56]

The *Western Union* case does not of necessity mean that a state may not use as a measure any elements of value or volume that would not be valid as a subject on which the tax is nominally imposed. There is one case in which the Supreme Court did not scrutinize a measure of net income too scrupulously because, as it let Mr. Justice Clarke say, the tax was not on net income.[57] Now that gross receipts from interstate sales may be directly taxed by the state of the buyer, at least in large part where the seller is sufficiently {196} ensconced there, they may of course be used as a measure.[58] But what about gross receipts from interstate transportation? The Court has reaffirmed the ancient law that gross receipts from transportation may not be made the direct subject of a state tax[59] except where the tax is one in lieu of a property tax and a fair substitute therefor.[60] So far as I know, the question whether gross receipts from interstate transportation may be made the measure of an excise on doing local business has received no clear answer.[61] Such a measure has not the due process vice of the measure of extraterritorial values. I wish I knew what the Supreme Court would do about it.

In the *Western Union* case the Court looked through a good subject to a bad measure and thus condemned. {197} Massachusetts had a tax on doing business measured by proper fractions of net income and of what Massachusetts calls the corporate excess, which clearly is without fault when imposed on doing local business. The Attorney General of Massachusetts once held that it might not be imposed on a foreign corporation engaged exclusively in interstate commerce. This had been established law—that there must be a valid subject. Solely from interest in theory, I urged that the issue be tested. It was tested, and the Supreme Court condemned the exaction in *Alpha Portland Cement Co. v. Massachusetts*,[62] Mr. Justice McReynolds asserting that "The amount demanded is unimportant when there is no legitimate basis for the tax."[63] I suggested that Massachusetts amend its statute to read: "This tax shall be imposed on the net income properly allocated to Massachusetts, or on doing business measured by the net income, whichever may make any particular levy more palatable to the Supreme Court of the United States."

My pernickety suggestion has not been adopted, and recently the *Spector* case[64] has followed the *Alpha Portland* case, and there must of course be some satisfactory justification for it. It doubtless is that for reasons of judicial administration the Court wishes to be satisfied by casual reading whether there is a traditionally good subject of the tax. But suppose a state passes a special statute confined to foreign corporations engaged exclusively in interstate commerce and puts the tax directly on an acceptable fraction of assets and net income. Property may be directly taxed though used in a business consisting exclusively of {198} interstate commerce,[65] and it has been said, though I believe that the Court has never had occasion to decide, that net income derived exclusively from interstate commerce is subject to state tax.[66] In any event, the property may be assessed at a capitalization of its earning power.[67] If the words of the statute are right, there are various ways of getting state sustenance from the contributions of interstate commerce. If the Court can look through a good subject and condemn for a bad measure, why can it not look through a bad subject and condone for a good measure?

In working with economists on reports for government commissions, I find them all inclined to write as the treasurer of a corporation would write. He dubs the exaction by what determines its amount. He knows property taxes, gross receipts taxes, and net income taxes, but with the law as it is, I made the economists be legalistic enough to say "on franchise," "on doing business," "on doing local business," "measured by," and so forth. This suggests the requirement that excises on doing business should read "excises on doing local business" to avoid possible difficulties. In *Leloup v. Port of Mobile*[68] in 1888 the Court condemned an annual, specific, non-admeasured tax of $225 on telegraph companies, because it was not clearly confined to doing local business, and the Western Union Telegraph Company engaged in both local and interstate transmission. This overruled a contrary decision of 1873 in *Osborne v. Mobile*.[69] {199} With a few spasmodic exceptions,[70] the issue rarely rose again, and I wondered after a time if it had been forgotten. My guess is that the state courts, knowing the law, interpreted state statutes by inserting the word "local" before "doing business" in order to avoid unconstitutionality, and so the question did not arise.[71]

Whether this was the explanation or not, Mr. Justice Brandeis in 1928 wrote the opinion in *Sprout v. South Bend*[72] condemning an annual license fee, graduated according to capacity, on a bus company engaged in mixed local and interstate transportation, not justifiable as compensation for the use of the highways. The reason given was that under the wording of the statute, the tax would be demandable even if the company were engaged exclusively in interstate commerce. A tax on gross receipts may be subdivided and part held good and part held bad,[73] but a specific demand is not thus splittable. One of the subsequent cases applying *Leloup v. Mobile* is *Cooney v. Mt. States Telephone Co.*,[74] condemning a bracketed tax on telephone instruments, starting at ten cents per phone for the first twenty and rising to a dollar per phone for all in excess of seventy-five. The instruments were used indiscriminately in local and interstate communication, and under the statute the fee would have been demandable under the statute for telephones used exclusively in interstate conversation. Therefore the tax was in part on interstate commerce {200} and no one could tell what part was on the taxable and what on the untaxable.

This may seem somewhat formal, and not less so when a condemned tax may be saved by insertion of the word "local" either by the state legislature or the state court.[75] Once it was suggested to the Supreme Court that the specific fee might be so large for the volume of local commerce that it must be deemed to take toll from interstate commerce. The Court agreed to stop, look, and listen. In the two cases in question,[76] however, the Court found the fees moderate and were not certain that the figures showed them to be disproportionate to the local business or that the low return on local business was certain to continue. This seems a questionable approach. Taxes on proper subjects may take toll from interstate commerce in various ways. The inquiry should be along the line of the *Western Union* case: Can the flat fee on doing local business be so disproportionate as to be deemed an assessment of extraterritorial business or values?[77] It must never be forgotten {201} that from the economic standpoint the states may tax interstate commerce and its fruits if they go about it in the right legal way.

This was recognized by that great lawyer and great advocate, James C. Carter, in his unsuccessful petition for a reargument of the decision sustaining an Ohio property tax on the reputed Ohio portion of the property of an express company represented by total capital stock.[78] Railroad property had with the approval of the Supreme Court been assessed by taking the total value and then taking the Ohio portion of it.[79] Railroads, however, have a physical unity. It was urged that express companies have no such unity. A horse is a horse, a wagon, a wagon, a desk, a desk, as Gertrude Stein might say. The Supreme Court held however that there was a unity of use and management, and it sustained an assessment of the Ohio value in the total capital stock that was greatly in excess of the physical value of the chattels located in Ohio. Of course the excess represented a moiety of the capitalization of earning power. As a concession Mr. Carter had written on the first hearing:

> There is one necessary exception to the rule that the States cannot tax interstate commerce. Inasmuch as the existence of the States is necessary to the existence of interstate commerce, that ordinary system of taxation which is necessary to the existence of the States, namely, taxation upon all property within them, must be permitted, and the property employed in interstate commerce is not to be exempted.[80]

{202} He then added that the exception was more apparent than real, because interstate commerce is not really burdened by taxation imposed on all property. If exempted, it would in effect be given a bonus.

Mr. Carter in effect contended that assessment by a capitalization of earning power is not universal. He was of course correct, but assessment of real estate takes account of a guess of what it would sell for, and what it would sell for takes account of a guess of what it would earn. The assessment of two bridges across the Mississippi river may vary greatly notwithstanding something approaching equality in the cost of their construction, but one bridge may have a remunerative, long-term contract for use by railroad trains, which the other may not.[81] The bridge itself is not more valuable than what it would cost to replace it, but the long-term contract with the railroad may be highly valuable. Earning power is not always incorporated in physical assets. A taxi enterprise may earn an income that is far higher than 6 or 10 percent of what it would cost to replace the ancient vehicles. Outside of taxing net income, there may be no way of assessing a capitalization of earning power owned by individuals. But such capitalization may be reached in the capital of a corporation, and it may be incorporated in choice corner lots. Interstate commerce may create values which states may assess and tax.

The major difficulty in state taxation of property and net income of far-flung transportation and industrial enterprises is that of allocating to each state its fair share of the national total. No factor and no combination of factors can {203} guarantee accurate allotments. From one standpoint this would not greatly matter if each state adopted identical criteria. A group of us who struggled to devise for Congressional adoption a single system for apportioning air line values among the states[82] achieved no marked success. This was undertaken after the Supreme Court had sanctioned a state property tax on the entire fleet of airplanes at the corporate and operational headquarters after refusal of assessors to grant reductions proportionate to the known absences of the planes on regular scheduled routes outside the state.[83] This decision has now been discounted by a Scotch verdict of "Not Proven," so that for the moment at least it is law that proper fractions of the value of migratory vehicles of transportation may be taxed away from home[84] and corresponding reductions may be secured for sufficiently regular absences from home.[85]

In the most recent decision on property taxation of airplanes Mr. Justice Frankfurter, in writing a dissenting essay on the subject, concludes by saying: "I am not unaware that there is an air of imprecision about what I have written. Such is the intention."[86] Imprecision is better than a delusive effort at precision, or than competing and contradictory delusive efforts for absolutes and generalities where particulars are so variegated in various respects. Airplanes present considerations different from those characteristic of railroads and telegraph systems, different also from those {204} of rolling stock owned by shipping groups and not by railroads. Various factors of allocation may not have the same appropriateness for property taxation of fixed instruments as for net income or gross income. Vessels roaming the sea present problems unlike canal boats and scows on fixed routes on inland rivers.[87] For railroads, and for telegraph and telephone communicators, line mileage is a less appropriate factor for allocation than is track mileage and wire mileage. Relative time of freight cars and airplanes in a state may be compared with actual miles of travel or with miles of the railroad over which the cars run or miles of air over which planes fly. Ten daily flights over a route are more significant than one a day or than an average of different flights on different days.[88] And what about stops and pickups and discharges of freight and passengers? Are they more important than miles of paid service or other miles? Do so-called bridge states merit any tax now that *jusque ad coelum* is modified?

Such are some of the problems for which the Constitution provides no definite answers and for which various Justices of the Supreme Court give varied ones. The rules as to vehicles differ from those applied to their contents and cargoes. This may be because the states have not worked out any scheme of averages for the presences within their borders of grain and coal and sheep and logs and oil and gas, as they have for cars and ships and planes. I should think that if the Court were presented with an appropriate state statute, it should permit the taxation of the right average {205} of oil in a pipe line as it does of tank cars. A state with a pipe line full of oil every day in the year ought to be able to assess what the pipe line holds, even if day by day new oil succeeds to old and every gallon moves continuously in an interstate stream. But it would hardly be appropriate to tax for a year coal or grain or livestock that is present for only a day. Yet the latter is permitted if the stop on tax day is deemed to be "for an independent local advantage."[89] If different states have different tax days and there are stops for independent local advantages in different states, movable chattels may be hit much harder than stationary ones.

Year by year oddities and sports in the botanical sense come to the Supreme Court for judgment and find diversities among the Justices. One of the latest is *Railway Express Agency v. Virginia*,[90] decided on April 5, 1954, by a five-to-four vote. The Railway Express Agency did no local business in Virginia except through a subsidiary. It confined itself to interstate commerce to escape from the grip of a Virginia statute requiring foreign corporations desiring to do certain kinds of local business to take out a Virginia charter and become *pro tanto* domesticated.[91] The quarrel in this case involved what the treasurer of the Agency would have been inclined to call a gross receipts tax of $66,454.71 which, at the statutory rate of levy, would be based on gross receipts from within the state amounting to $3,090,916.55. {206} The Agency had not theretofore contested the amount, assumed to be the share of the national gross receipts from the transmission of interstate express within the borders of Virginia. So the dispute boiled down to whether the tax was on the privilege of engaging in interstate commerce or whether the receipts were taken to represent the going concern value of the Agency in Virginia.

The tangible property of the Agency in Virginia was assessed at $129,279. Mr. Justice Jackson said that "To ascribe a going-concern value of over three million dollars to tangible property of $129,279 is on its face an extreme attribution."[92] The legislature had called the tax a license tax on doing business. The State Commission and state court were aware that this made the tax unconstitutional under the *Spector* case,[93] so they renamed the tax as one on intangible going-concern value. The majority of the Supreme Court rejected this characterization. The minority, consisting of Mr. Justice Clark, who spoke for them, and of Mr. Chief Justice Warren and Justices Black and Douglas, accepted the revised nomenclature and would sustain the tax. Two of the dissenters had been legal officers in their home states, and the other two were normally pro-tax minded. The dispute was about what the tax was really on, as the dissent did not insist that a tax directly on gross receipts from interstate carriage is constitutional. Doubtless unexpressed considerations of desirability and undesirability entered into processes of reaching these diverse judgments, though of course these are not appropriate for judicial consideration. The answers must be dictated by the document of 1787. {207}

Even where the Constitution says something about state taxation, it leaves a good bit undecided. Subject to a qualification about inspection fees it says that "No State shall, without the Consent of the Congress, lay any Imposts or Duties on Imports or Exports. . . ."[94] And with respect to Congress it says: "No Tax or Duty shall be laid on Articles exported from any State."[95] We saw from *Brown v. Maryland*[96] that it is a duty on an Import to put a tax on its first sale, if in the orignal package. *Low v. Austin*[97] in 1872 held that subjection to a general property tax is within the prohibition. *Hooven & Allison Co. v. Evatt*[98] applied the prohibition to a property tax on hemp in a warehouse awaiting processing into rope. Marshall recognized that the import ceases to be an import when "used." In dissenting in the Hemp case, Mr. Justice Black paraphrases this concession by saying "held for use."[99] Held in the factory for processing is closer to the introduction than is sale, which Marshall regarded as a nontaxable subject. Mr. Justice Black contends that Mr. Chief Justice Stone in declaring the hemp awaiting processing to be immune "interprets Marshall's opinion in a manner which squarely conflicts with his own interpretation of the rule he announced."[100] This is unacceptable, but it illustrates how Justices may differ.

There is a significant contrast in the application of the constitutional bans on Congress and on the states with respect to the taxation of exports and of goods going to sister states, which is hardly explainable by a difference in the wording of the two clauses. Delivery by the seller in the {208} seller's state does not make the sale interstate although the buyer comes in from a sister state to receive his purchase and then immediately takes it back home.[101] This had been applied earlier when the buyer of gasoline immediately took it to fishing boats on the high seas with a phony accompanying bill of lading that sought to make the buyer a mere shipper from the seller to the fishing fleet.[102] For all that appeared at the time, the ruling on receipt by the buyer in the seller's state would be followed if the buyer came in from Canada instead of from a sister state, at least as far as state taxation is concerned. The law as to state police power then differed in the two cases on grain deliveries in North Dakota[103] and Kentucky,[104] but the distinction could have been explained as one between police power and taxation in the state of a purchase for subsequent but speedy hauling to a sister state, and no problem of ultimate destination to a foreign country was involved.

However, in *Richfield Oil Corp. v. State Board*[105] in 1946, delivery of gasoline by a California vendor to a tanker sent in by the New Zealand government to receive it was held to be a sale for export and so not subject to the state sales tax. This would clearly be an article exported from the state if the shipment were by common carrier, but so it would be an interstate sale if delivered by common carrier to a sister state. So the difference between these two cases in which the buyer comes in from a sister state or comes {209} in from abroad must be a difference between the application of the commerce clause and that of the export clause. Mr. Justice Douglas hints at the distinction when he says that the scope of the limitation found in the commerce clause "has been determined by the Court in an effort to maintain an area of trade free from state interference and at the same time to make interstate commerce pay its way."[106] Trade from the United States to foreign countries is protected from having to pay its way both against Congress and against the states, because the two export clauses apply to foreign trade as by reinterpretation they do not apply to sales to buyers in sister states. Yet now even the commerce clause forbids a tax on what is conceded to be a sale to a sister state.[107] The difference in the law is between what is delivery to a sister state and what is delivery to a foreign country.

In condemning the tax on the sale of gasoline delivered in California to the tanker of the New Zealand government, Mr. Justice Douglas invokes the decision in *Spalding & Bros. v. Edwards*[108] which very likely would not be followed in the case of a state tax on a similar sale to a sister state and not to a foreign government. In the *Spalding* case a South American retailer asked a New York commission house to buy and ship athletic supplies to it. The commission concern selected the goods at Spalding's, got from them a bill of lading made out to the South American retailer. sent the bill of lading with draft attached to a South {210} American bank, with instructions to deliver the bill of lading to the South American retailer upon its honoring the draft. Spalding did not look to the South American retailer for the price. Their vendee from a commercial standpoint was the New York commission house to whom they gave the bill of lading. It could hardly matter whether the commission house was considered to have made its profit by a commission from Spalding or by a discount from the list price for which it made out its draft sent to the South American bank.

On the basis of the only facts related thus far, it would seem that Spalding made a local sale to the commission house, and the commission house sold for export to the South American retailer. There are two sales, but not two sales for export. The further fact, however, is that the commission house had Spalding arrange to ship the supplies straight to South America. Spalding did the manual exporting but not the commercial exporting, because the balls and bats and masks and gloves were under the control of the commission house through its control of the bill of lading. Nevertheless the Supreme Court saved Spalding from the Congressional excise on sales of athletic goods. In the New Zealand case, Mr. Justice Douglas quotes Mr. Justice Holmes in the *Spalding* case for the remarks that the issue was "whether the sale was a step in exportation"[109] and that "theoretical possibilities may be left out of account."[110] The latter reference is presumably to the possibility that the commission house might get possession of the goods by recovering the bill of lading if the draft were dishonored. {211} If Mr. Justice Holmes seems cavalier and not overly addicted to nicety, the result may still be acceptable.

In the Constitutional Convention of 1787, the delegates from states in which cotton, tobacco, and some other products were produced in greater quantities than could be consumed in this country were fearful of a national power to distribute the national fiscal burdens predominantly on trade in staple crops. The inclusion of this restriction on the national commerce and taxing powers was a price that had to be paid for acquiescence in the grant of these powers to Congress, or was at any rate assumed to be. The words "No Tax or Duty on Articles exported" were vague enough and therefore broad enough to cover a variety of taxes and a variety of points at which such taxes might impinge. The reasons behind the bargain which inserted the clause were such that it is appropriate to give weight to economic considerations as well as to literary or technical legal ones. For much of exportation by concerns not large enough to have foreign branches to stimulate orders, an American intermediary may be essential to shop around and meet the needs of foreign buyers not large enough to have resident purchasing agents here. This may warrant the decision in the *Spalding* case.

This judicial instinct to protect the exporting process from national fiscal demands finds expression in other cases having better warrant in economics than in language. Illustrations may be reported by quoting Mr. Justice Van Devanter in an opinion differentiating net income taxes from those that have been condemned. Of the extent of the restriction in favor of exports, he says: {212}

> The decisions of this court answer that it excepts from the range of [the taxing] power articles in course of exportation, *Turpin v. Burgess*, 117 U.S. 504, 507; the act or occupation of exporting, *Brown v. Maryland*, 12 Wheat. 419, 445; bills of lading for articles being exported, *Fairbank v. United States*, 181 U.S. 283; charter parties for the carriage of cargoes from state to foreign ports, *United States v. Hvoslef*, 237 U.S. 1; and policies of marine insurance on articles being exported—such insurance being uniformly regarded as "an integral part of the exportation" and the policy as "one of the ordinary shipping documents," *Thames and Mersey Insurance Co. v. United States*, 237 U.S. 19. In short, the court has interpreted the clause as meaning that exportation must be free from taxation, and therefore as requiring "not simply an omission of a tax upon the articles exported, but also a freedom from any tax which *directly* burdens the exportation."[111]

With this broad immunity, it is perhaps fortunate that Mr. Justice Miller and his colleagues held that interstate trade and transportation are not exportation. The national internal revenue laws now successfully reach not a little transportation and communication and documents facilitating them that would be outside their reach if Marshall's dictum about imports from a sister state had remained law.

This is the close of the appointed series, though there are various other fields of constitutional law that might be surveyed for further elaboration of my theme of "Our Undulant Constitution," which was my initially conceived title. This sounded somewhat like a fever, and "undulating" would have been more descriptive than "undulant." The most serious area of constitutional law not covered by this cursory survey is that of constitutional restrictions in favor of liberty and property. This includes due process restrictions {213} against both Congress and the states, the equal protection and the obligation of contracts barriers against state discriminations and retroactive frustration of public and private contracts, the special fields of civil liberties and procedures of criminal prosecution applicable with respect both to the states and to the nation, the distribution of power between three departments of government, limitations on state and national taxation, and a few others. If this were a treatise, all these and more would have to be covered. Police power is perhaps the most serious omission, but the decisions so obviously support and exemplify my thesis that they would afford an instance of *res ipsa loquitur*.

I am not one who favors the reporting of constitutional law by invoking the various constitutional clauses as chapter headings. The dictionary method of cataloguing the meaning of words seems to me undesirable when various clauses may bear upon the same issue and when it is not the meaning of words that usually determines the decisions. The decisions may in some cases determine the meaning of words, but usually with this are often intertwined issues of public policy, and analysis of intricate practicalities in fields outside the law to which the law must be applied. An interesting approach to the classifications of constitutional determinations by the judiciary is that of Hugh Evander Willis, formerly Professor of Law in the University of Indiana, who takes Dean Pound's classification of interests, such as the security of transactions, and under each heading gives first the common law regulations, then the statutory ones and the judicial pronouncements on the constitutionality of the statutes.[112] I used to think of the {214} due process clause as a prescription of anarchy, a realm of no-law. This was wrong. It may be the creation of zones into which executives and legislators may not enter or many enter only in certain ways, but it should be borne in mind that without statutes much of human conduct would be subject to common-law restrictions, though the methods of enforcing them would often be spasmodic and cumbrous.

This study of vagaries, variations, and irregularities in the constitutional law manufactured by the judges should not close without mention of others on which judges have never passed. The first has to do with the written word. The Articles of Confederation provided that the union created thereby should be perpetual and that no change should be made therein except by the vote of the Congress and ratification by the legislatures of all the thirteen states.[113] The Framers provided that the proposed Constitution should go into effect after ratification by conventions in nine of the thirteen states.[114] I at one time assumed that ratification by conventions instead of by legislatures rendered the Constitution forever unconstitutional under the Articles of Confederation. I have since changed my mind. The legislatures participated by calling the conventions, one somewhat belatedly. Congress approved of transmission to the states though rather *pro forma*. But the national government was organized before Rhode Island and North Carolina ratified. This was secession by eleven states. The Constitution did not become constitutional until the other two states duly ratified. It then became constitutional {215} even though the ratification was somewhat the fruit of coercion.

Even though all the thirteen original states duly ratified the Constitution in form, there was enough economic coercion on Rhode Island and

North Carolina to make their adhesion far from their wholly free will. Also, in the aftermath of the War between the States, there was complete coercion to secure ratification of the Fourteenth Amendment from the six unreconstructed states. They were not to be represented in Congress until they ratified, and the legislatures that ratified were chosen by an electorate with qualifications and disqualifications specified by Congress and administered by military governors. Even if the end might have been achieved by wholly disregarding these southern states, that was not the method chosen. Another blot on the constitutional escutcheon is the assumed consent of Virginia to the creation of West Virginia as an independent state. One might even suggest that the separation of the thirteen colonies from the mother country contained elements of the extralegal. Fortunately, even in tracing the titles of real estate, there is not infrequently needed the saving grace of prescription. Prescription may need to be invoked in making acceptable the course of constitutional history and of constitutional law.

Notes

1 *See, e.g.,* The Passenger Cases, 7 How. 283 (1849); Case of the State Freight Tax, 15 Wall. 232 (1873); Robbins v. Shelby County Taxing District, 120 U.S. 489 (1887).

2 *See, e.g.,* State Tax on Railway Gross Receipts, 15 Wall. 284 (1873); Horn Silver Mining Co. v. New York, 143 U.S. 305 (1892).

3 Cooley v. Board of Port Wardens, 12 How. 299 (1851).

4 Pennsylvania Gas Co. v. Public Service Comm., 252 U.S. 23 (1920).

5 East Ohio Gas Co. v. Tax Comm., 283 U.S. 465 (1931).

6 12 Wheat. 419 (1827).

7 *Id.* at 441-42, 443.

8 May v. New Orleans, 178 U.S. 496 (1900).

9 12 Wheat, at 446-49.

10 9 Wheat. 1 (1824).

11 12 Wheat, at 449.

12 8 Wall. 123 (1869).

13 *Id.* at 139, 140.

14 *Id.* at 136-37.

15 *Id.* at 137.

16 12 Wheat. at 443.

17 Leisy v. Hardin, 135 U.S. 100 (1890); Schollenberger v. Pennsylvania, 171 U.S. 1 (1898).

18 114 U.S. 622.

19 Hooven & Allison Co. v. Evatt, 324 U.S. 652 (1945).

20 171 U.S. 345.

21 Red "C" Oil Mfg. Co. v. Board of Agriculture, 222 U.S. 380 (1912); Savage v. Jones, 225 U.S. 501 (1912); Standard Stock Food Co. v. Wright, 225 U.S. 540 (1912); Pure Oil Co. v. Minnesota, 248 U.S. 158 (1918).

22 Standard Oil Co. v. Graves, 249 U.S. 389 (1919); Askren v. Continental Oil Co., 252 U.S. 444 (1920); Texas Co. v. Brown, 258 U.S. 466 (1922).

23 Wagner v. Covington, 251 U.S. 95 (1919).

24 262 U.S. 506.

25 *Id.* at 520.

26 *Id.* at 520.

27 *Id.* at 515.

28 120 U.S. 489.

29 327 U.S. 416.

30 Banker Bros. Co. v. Pennsylvania, 222 U.S. 210 (1911).

31 Norfolk & Western Ry. v. Sims, 191 U.S. 441 (1903).

32 Rearick v. Pennsylvania, 203 U.S. 507 (1906).

33 203 U.S. at 512.

34 Adams Mfg. Co. v. Storen, 304 U.S. 307 (1938); Gwin, White & Prince, Inc. v. Henneford, 305 U.S. 434 (1939).

35 Wiloil Corp. v. Pennsylvania, 294 U.S. 169 (1935).

36 309 U.S. 33.

37 *Id.* at 55.

38 Wiloil Corp. v. Pennsylvania, *supra* n. 35; Graybar Electric Co. v. Curry, 308 U.S. 513 (1939).

39 Henneford v. Silas Mason Co., 300 U.S. 577 (1937). *Cf.* Gregg Dyeing Co. v. Query, 286 U.S. 472 (1932).

40 329 U.S. 249.

41 *But see* Michigan Business Receipts Tax (Act No. 150, Michigan Public Acts of 1953), § 3 (1) (b).

42 *Cf.* Heisler v. Thomas Colliery Co., 260 U.S. 245 (1922).

43 McGoldrick v. Berwind-White Coal Mining Co., 309 U.S. 33 (1940).

44 Nelson v. Sears, Roebuck & Co., 312 U.S. 359 (1951).

45 McLeod v. Dilworth Co., 322 U.S. 327 (1944).

46 General Trading Co. v. State Tax Comm., 322 U.S. 335 (1944).

47 The situation giving rise to co-existence of nonliability for a sales tax with liability for collection of a use tax may be narrower than first appeared. General Trading Co. v.

State Tax Comm., *supra* n. 46, appears to have been substantially qualified by the more recent and more closely divided decision in Miller Bros. Co. v. Maryland, 347 U.S. 340 (1954). In the former case Mr. Justice Jackson, speaking only for himself and Mr. Justice Roberts in dissent, said, "So we [*i.e.*, the majority] are holding that a state has power to make a tax collector of one whom it has no power to tax." (322 U.S. at 339.) In the latter case, holding that a Delaware department store which sent no selling agents into Maryland could not be required to collect and remit the Maryland use tax on store sales to Maryland residents, even when sale was followed by delivery, the same Justice, now enjoying the support of four colleagues, remarked, "It would be a strange law that would make appellant more vulnerable to liability for another's tax than to a tax on itself." (347 U.S. at 346.)

48 United States Glue Co. v. Town of Oak Creek, 247 U.S. 321 (1918); Peck & Co. v. Lowe, 247 U.S. 165 (1918).

49 *See, e.g.,* Underwood Typewriter Co. v. Chamberlain, 254 U.S. 113 (1920); Bass, Ratcliff & Gretton v. State Tax Comm., 266 U.S. 271 (1924); Hans Rees' Sons v. North Carolina, 283 U.S. 123 (1931).

50 Norfolk & Western Ry. v. North Carolina, 297 U.S. 682 (1936).

51 216 U.S. 1.

52 St. Louis S.W. Ry. v. Arkansas, 235 U.S. 350 (1914).

53 91 US. 275 (1876).

54 See Harlan, J., 216 U.S. at 27, 33, 37 and 47-48. *Cf.* concurring opinion of White, C.J. at 50-51.

55 Baltic Mining Co. v. Massachusetts, 231 U.S. 68 (1913).

56 Albert Pick & Co. v. Jordan, 169 Calif. 1, 24, 145 Pac. 506, 515 (1915).

57 Hump Hairpin Mfg. Co. v. Emmerson, 258 U.S. 290 (1922).

58 Norton Co. v. Dept. of Revenue, 340 U.S. 534 (1951).

59 Joseph v. Carter & Weekes Stevedoring Co., 330 U.S. 422 (1947). Whether this decision was sharply limited by Central Greyhound Lines, Inc. v. Mealey, 334 U.S. 653 (1948), appears to depend upon the scope to be attributed to the latter decision. For apparently conflicting appraisals of its significance, see Douglas, J., in Canton R.R. v. Rogan, 340 U.S. 511, at 515-16 (1951), and Burton, J., in Spector Motor Service, Inc. v. O'Connor, 340 U.S. 602, at 610 (1951). *Cf.* Michigan-Wisconsin Pipe Line Co. v. Calvert, 347 U.S. 157 (1954).

60 Cudahy Packing Co. v. Minnesota, 246 U.S. 450 (1918); Great Northern Ry. v. Minnesota, 278 U.S. 503 (1929).

61 Both the four-one-four division of the Court and the nature of Justice Burton's solo opinion render inconclusive the decision in Interstate Oil Pipe Line Co. v. Stone, 337 U.S. 662 (1949). Nor does Canton R.R. v. Rogan, 340 U.S. 511 (1951), necessarily give an answer. The Court of Appeals of Maryland (195 Md. 206, 73 A. 2d 12) treated the tax as one imposed in lieu of a property tax within the rule of the decisions in note 60 *supra*. Moreover, the corporation was a domestic corporation, and since the *Western Union* case the Court has regularly employed a double standard in appraising the measure of franchise taxes for domestic as against foreign corporations. *See* Cream of Wheat Co. v. County of Grand Fork, 253 U.S. 325 (1920); Nebraska *ex rel.* Beatrice Creamery Co. v. Marsh, 282 U.S. 799 (1930).

62 268 U.S. 203 (1925).

63 *Id.* at 218.

64 Spector Motor Service, Inc. v. O'Connor, 340 U.S. 602 (1951).

65 Henderson Bridge Co. v. Kentucky, 166 U.S. 150 (1897).

66 See Stone, C.J., in Memphis Natural Gas Co. v. Beeler, 315 U.S. 649, 656 (1942). *But cf.* Roy Stone Transfer Corp. v. Messner, 377 Penn. 234, 103 A. 2d 700 (1954).

67 St. Louis, etc., Ry. v. Missouri, 256 U.S. 314 (1921); Henderson Bridge Co. v. Kentucky, *supra* n. 65

68 127 U.S. 640.

69 16 Wall. 479.

70 Allen v. Pullman's Palace Car Co., 191 U.S. 171 (1903). *Cf.* Postal Telegraph Co. v. Adams, 155 U.S. 688 (1895).

71 *Cf.* Raley & Bros. v. Richardson, 264 U.S. 157 (1924).

72 277 U.S. 163.

73 Ratterman v. Western Union Tel. Co., 127 U.S. 411 (1888).

74 294 U.S. 384 (1935).

75 The rule of the *Leloup* and *Sprout* cases may recently have passed from formalism into history. In Chicago v. Willett Co., 344 U.S. 574 (1953), the Court, in an opinion by Mr. Justice Frankfurter, upheld a Chicago license tax on trucks, as applied to trucks engaged in both local and interstate operations. Mr. Justice Douglas dissented, asserting conflict with the *Sprout* decision. On the same day, in Bode v. Barrett, 344 U.S. 583 (1953), the majority of the Court, in an opinion by Mr. Justice Douglas, upheld an Illinois license tax on trucks, as applied to trucks engaged in both local and interstate operations. From this decision, Mr. Justice Frankfurter dissented, asserting conflict with the *Leloup* decision. From this apparent contest of loyalties to *Leloup* and *Sprout*, those decisions may have emerged shorn of their authority. See Note, *The Supreme Court, 1952 Term,* 67 HARV. L. REV. 91, 125-28.

76 Allen v. Pullman's Palace Car Co., *supra* n. 70; Pullman Co. v. Adams, 189 U.S. 420 (1903).

77 *Cf.* Pacific Tel. & Tel. Co. v. Tax Comm., 297 U.S. 403 (1936).

78 Adams Express Co. v. Ohio State Auditor, 166 U.S. 185 (1897).

79 Cleveland, C.C. & St. L. Ry. v. Backus, 154 U.S. 439 (1894).

80 Adams Express Co. v. Ohio State Auditor, 165 U.S. 194, 217-18 (1897).

81 See Brewer, J., in the *Adams Express* case, *supra* n. 78, 166 U.S. at 219-20.

82 MULTIPLE TAXATION OF AIR COMMERCE, HOUSE DOC. No. 141, 79th Congress, 1st Sess. (1945).

83 Northwest Airlines v. Minnesota, 322 U.S. 292 (1944).

84 Braniff Airways, Inc. v. Nebraska State Board, 347 U.S. 590 (1954).

85 *Cf.* Standard Oil Co. v. Peck, 342 U.S. 382 (1952).

86 347 U.S. at 609.

87 *Cf.* Southern Pacific Co. v. Kentucky, 222 U.S. 63 (1911), *with* Ott v. Mississippi Valley Barge Line Co., 336 U.S. 169 (1949), and Standard Oil Co. v. Peck, *supra* n. 85.

88 *Cf.* Union Tank Line Co. v. Wright, 249 U.S. 275 (1919).

89 Minnesota v. Blasius, 290 U.S. 1 (1933), and cases therein cited.

90 347 U.S. 359.

91 For litigation over this requirement and comment on its significance see Railway Express Agency, Inc. v. Virginia, 282 U.S. 440 (1931), and Note, *Compulsory Incorporation and the Power to Tax,* 44 HARV. L. REV. 1111.

92 347 U.S. at 366.

93 *Supra* n. 64.

94 U.S. CONST. ART. I, § 10.

95 U.S. CONST. ART. I, § 9.

96 *Supra* n. 6.

97 13 Wall. 29.

98 *Supra* n. 19.

99 324 U.S. at 687, 689 and 690.

100 *Id.* at 687.

101 Department of Treasury v. Wood Preserving Corp., 313 U.S. 62 (1941).

102 Superior Oil Co. v. Mississippi, 280 U.S. 390 (1930).

103 Lemke v. Farmers Grain Co., 258 U.S. 50 (1922).

104 Dahnke-Walker Milling Co. v. Bondurant, 257 U.S. 282 (1921).

105 329 U.S. 69.

106 *Id.* at 75.

107 Adams Mfg. Co. v. Storen, 304 U.S. 307 (1938); Freeman v. Hewit, 329 U.S. 249 (1946).

108 262 U.S. 66 (1923).

109 *Id.* at 68.

110 *Id.* at 70.

111 Peck & Co. v. Lowe, 247 U.S. 165, 173 (1918).

112 WILLIS, CONSTITUTIONAL LAW OF THE UNITED STATES.

113 ARTICLES OF CONFEDERATION, Art. XIII.

114 U.S. CONST., Art. VII.

Index

Page numbers below reference the original pagination, embedded into the text of this modern edition by the use of {brackets}. See 'Notes of the Series Editor.'

ꟼl₽

Visit us at *www.quidprobooks.com*.